ENCOUNTERS WITH CHRIST

ENCOUNTERS WITH CHRIST
Introduction to the Sacraments

William P. Roberts

PAULIST PRESS
New York/Mahwah

Acknowledgments

All biblical quotations are taken from *The Jerusalem Bible* unless otherwise indicated. The letters NAB at the end of a reference refer to the *New American Bible*.

Excerpts from the English translation of the *Rite of Marriage* © 1970, International Committee on English in the Liturgy, Inc. (ICEL); excerpts from the English translation of *The Roman Missal* © 1973, ICEL; excerpts from the English translation of the *Rite of Penance* © 1974, ICEL; excerpts from the English translation of the *Rite of Christian Initiation of Adults* © 1974, 1978, ICEL; excerpts from the English translation of the *Ordination of Deacons, Priests, and Bishops* © 1976, ICEL; excerpts from the English translation of *Pastoral Care of the Sick: Rites of Anointing and Viaticum* © 1982, ICEL. All rights reserved.

Library of Congress
Catalog Card Number: 85-60297

ISBN: 0-8091-2707-5

Published by Paulist Press
997 Macarthur Boulevard
Mahwah, N.J. 07430

Printed and bound in the United States of America

Contents

With the belief that sacramentality is experienced
first and foremost in the context of family,
I lovingly dedicate this book to
my wife Challon
and
our daughters
Carolyn, Laura and Kathryn

Foreword

When Robert Heyer, formerly of Paulist Press, suggested that I write this book, my first reaction was one of reluctance. With the recent flurry of good books on the sacraments, do we need another? The decision to write this volume was finally made in order to provide an introductory text that can be used in a general college or advanced senior high level course on the sacraments. This book is also designed for use in parish adult religious education programs and for general readership.

The first section of the book studies the meaning of sacrament in general. The remaining sections treat of each of the seven sacraments. The main purpose throughout the book is to bring together key contemporary biblical and theological insights that can provide a better understanding and appreciation of the sacraments and the meaning they can have for living a more committed Christian life.

To help achieve this purpose, the book is written in a deliberately non-technical way. While footnotes are omitted, a list of suggested further readings is provided at the end of the book. To aid in the process of personally integrating the material, questions for reflection and discussion are included at the end of each chapter.

I wish to express my thanks to my wife, Challon, for her encouragement and help throughout the writing of this manuscript. I am also grateful to Robert Heyer for the inspiration in undertaking this endeavor, and to Rev. Kevin Lynch, C.S.P. and Robert Hamma, editors at Paulist Press for their continued support and guidance. Finally, a word of thanks to Joanne Beirise and Elaine Eichman for typing the entire work.

Part One

FOUNDATIONAL INSIGHTS

One of the problems with understanding sacramental theology has been the tendency to isolate the sacraments from human experience and from the rest of Christian life. This first section of the book strives to situate the sacraments in such a context. To accomplish this we first reflect on the experience of human friendship and how words and signs function in establishing our personal relationships with one another. We then look at the God-human relationship and probe how God has communicated to humans through words and signs. Chapters 3 and 4 focus on Christ as the fundamental sacrament, and on the Church as the sacrament of Christ.

Chapter 1
Word, Sign and Friendship

Friendship is an essential component of human life. Precisely what distinguishes humans from the remainder of the animal kingdom is the ability to share mind and heart and to enter into communion with one another. It is because of this gift that humans are described as being made in the image and likeness of God.

Personal friendships are, therefore, sacramental of who God is for humans. It is significant that in the Hebrew scriptures God is described in terms of two of the most intimate human relationships, marriage and parenthood. God is perceived as the faithful husband of Israel. God's love is compared to that of a father and mother.

In this chapter we probe the meaning of human friendship and examine some of its components. We will then point to some of the practical implications that an understanding of human friendship has for a meaningful approach to sacraments.

Human Friendships

We are conceived and born in the context of personal relationship. From the earliest stages of our existence we are shaped and influenced in terms of the quality of the relationships we experience with other people, first our parents, and then our siblings and friends.

A friendship is formed when two people freely give and receive the gift of themselves to each other. This self-gift needs to be expressed in many ways. Basically, we communicate with each other through words and signs. Words explain what is on our mind and in our heart. Through words people say what they mean to each other. Words express our love and esteem, our aspirations and desires, our compassion and forgiveness.

Words, however, can be cheap. They need to be supported by action and signs. It is not enough to tell others that we love them. We must show it. Signs, whether an embrace, a gift, or a ring, help indicate that we mean what we say. Signs or symbols reinforce our words. They also express feelings that we cannot adequately verbalize.

On the other hand, words are needed to explain the sign. Flowers left at one's door have some meaning in themselves. But in order for the flowers to speak one's love or one's congratulations, or one's sympathy, a signed card needs to be attached. While we can distinguish between words and signs, it is important to note that words themselves have a sign dimension. They are verbal signs of our inner thoughts. Signs, on the other hand, have a word dimension. They, indeed, communicate a message. Words and signs, then, are not in opposition. Rather they complement each other. Together they enable us to communicate our deeper selves. The power that words and signs have to transform us and bind us together depends on the degree of the gift of ourselves to one another. Who we are for one another, and how personally present we are willing to be for another, are the critical realities. Words and signs only derive their power from the meaning we give to them.

Practical Implications

These brief reflections on human friendship and on how word and sign function in personal communication can shed light on the divine-human relationship and on the role sacraments can play in God's communication to humans. Several specific points can be highlighted here.

1. The foundation of the divine-human communication is God's self-gift to humans. God first reveals himself. Under the impact of this divine self-communication, humans are empowered to respond to God in faith and love. What is called the life of grace is precisely this friendship that exists between God and the human. This relationship, this life of grace grows as any friendship does, namely through communication and response.

Grace, then, is not a quantitative thing. Hence, it does not grow as a quantity does. The life of grace grows in terms of our deepening communion with God in faith, trust and love.

2. Sacraments are signs of the personal presence and self-gift of God and Christ. They are not things. Hence, before children are taught about the sacraments, they need to be introduced to God as a concerned and loving being, who is with us in all the realities of daily living. They need to be introduced to Christ as a friend. Children need to have some appreciation of how God and Christ manifest their goodness and love to them in human relationships, and in the beauties of nature.

3. The words of scripture and the sacraments complement each other. God speaks to us through the scriptures. Through sacramental actions God manifests God's love and involvement in our lives.

4. Sacraments are first and foremost gifts offered by God and Christ, and not legal obligations imposed on people. It is unfortunate that for centuries Catholic education and spiritual

formation has so often insisted on the latter rather than emphasizing the former. If the life of grace as friendship with Christ is stressed, then it is easy to see the sacraments as gifts of love. Christians are called to respond to these gifts and thus grow in friendship with God. Sacraments are important ways of growing in faith and love, and cannot be reduced to legal obligations. If in human friendship preparing meals, embracing and kissing, and the giving and receiving of gifts become primarily burdensome obligations, serious trouble in the relationship is indicated. If sacraments are approached primarily as obligation, what does this say about our relationship with Christ?

5. In human friendship the quality of our actions is of greater significance than merely the number of times we perform them. Some acts of love need to be repeated on a regular basis: changing diapers, providing transportation, saying "I love you." But the value these actions have for bonding people together in genuine understanding and love depend on the way in which they are done and the motivation behind them. Actions that are done begrudgingly, with resentment, or with a "no care" attitude can actually have an alienating effect. Only to the degree in which even these "routine" actions are done with concern, kindness and sensitivity do they deepen our relationship with another.

The same principle applies to "special" actions which we perform. The number of times one takes his wife out to dinner or sends her flowers has some pertinence. But it is not the primary issue. What these actions represent in terms of the quality of the relationship is of greater significance.

While this insight is easily acknowledged in respect to human relationships, it somehow has gotten lost when we approach the sacraments. Too often the question of foremost concern has been "How many times do you go to confession?" or "How frequently do you attend Mass?" Far less concern was manifested regarding the quality of the experience and the effect the sacrament had on one's relationship with Christ and with others. It was presupposed that "more was better" because somehow sacraments "automatically gave grace" regardless of the quality of the experience.

The value that sacraments have for one's faith life depends on the quality of one's ongoing relationship with Christ. It also depends on one's faith understanding, and to some degree, at least, on the way the sacrament is celebrated. One cannot, then, measure the value of sacraments merely in terms of number. It is necessary to evaluate what participation in the sacrament is really doing to one's relationship with God, Christ, and one's fellow humans.

Summary

To be in the "the state of grace" is to be in openness to God's friendship. Human beings grow in friendship with each other by exchanging a variety of verbal and symbolic communications. Friendship with God is nurtured by being responsive to God's self-gift in word and sacrament.

Some of the principles that are operative in human relationship can guide our approach to sacraments. It is especially important that the action of Christ in sacraments be perceived primarily as gracious gift rather than a legal burden. It is also essential that there be less concentration on the mere number of times in which sacraments are received, and more stress on the personal quality of the celebration.

REFLECTION/DISCUSSION QUESTIONS

1. Why is the experience of human friendship one of the best ways of coming to an understanding of the relationship between God and humans?

2. Reflect on a meaningful friendship you have had with an-
    other person. Describe how that relationship helped you
    become a better person and enriched your life.
3. How do word and sign function in our ordinary human in-
    terchange with one another?
4. How can reflecting on the way human friendship grows aid
    in a meaningful approach to sacraments?

Chapter 2
Word and Sign in Scripture

To understand further God's present self-communication to us through word and sign, it will be helpful to recall briefly the pattern of God's communication as recorded in the scriptures. In the first part of the chapter we look at God's self-revelation to the Israelite people through word and sign. We then reflect on Jesus' own proclamation of the kingdom of God through word and sign in his public ministry.

God and Israel

The Old Testament reveals the history of God's self-revelation to Israel, and of the response the people of Israel made to God. The library of diverse books that constitute the Old Testament record some of the significant works that God performed on behalf of the people. They also contain the word of God revealed to the people through prophetic and charismatic leaders. In order for God's actions to be signs of God's loving and faithful covenant with Israel, they needed to be interpreted in faith and explained to the people. Thus interpreted and explained, the works of the Lord became powerful symbols that manifested to the people the seriousness and permanence of God's love and involvement.

To illustrate how God's works and the revealed word complement each other in the Old Testament account, we will cite three examples: the creation, the passover event, and the return of the exiles from Babylon.

Apart from faith, the works of creation tell us nothing about God. Even if philosophers can "prove" the existence of God by arguing that the wonders of the universe presuppose a supreme being, they cannot lead us to know God in faith and in personal relationship.

In order for the wonders of creation to be attributed to One who loves us, cares for us, and is involved in our lives, God must reveal God's self to us and empower us to believe. Because God spoke to the Israelite people and revealed the convenantal love God had for them, they were able to see the hand of God in all creation.

The various creation accounts in the Old Testament, then, do not pretend to be newspaper reports nor scientific explanations. They are proclamations of faith. The visible realities of the universe became signs in faith of the wonders of the Lord and of God's abiding covenantal love. Through this faith perception of the created universe, the Israelites grew in their belief that their God was a God of life. They came to trust that this God would not abandon them.

The historical event that became the most significant sign of God's covenant with Israel was the deliverance from Egypt in the thirteenth century B.C. The Israelites had been enslaved by the Egyptians. To those without faith, the escape of the Israelites from slavery could be explained merely in political terms.

However, through God's revelation to Moses, the exodus from Egypt took on a whole new significance. It was God who was concerned about the miserable state of the Israelites. God raised up Moses and commissioned him to lead the Israelites out of Egypt. It was God who made possible the extraordinary deliverance from slavery, and who led the people to freedom in the promised land.

In faith the Israelites celebrated this event in the passover meal. They gathered to eat the passover lamb and unleavened bread. During the meal the story was retold of how the God of the covenant did not forget the chosen people, but looked upon them in their misery and brought them to the promised land.

No historical event in the Old Testament tested the faith of the Jews more than the downfall of the kingdom of Judah in 587 B.C. The Babylonians destroyed the city of Jerusalem and the temple. They had deported many of the inhabitants to Babylon. For almost half a century the Jews remained in exile. Finally, in 539 B.C. the armies of Cyrus, king of the Medes and Persians, entered Babylon. After conquering the Babylonians, Cyrus issued an edict allowing the return of the exiles to Judah.

On the surface, the victory of Cyrus over the Babylonians could be seen merely as another political conquest due to the superiority of Cyrus' military prowess. His edict allowing the return of the exiles could be explained in terms of humanitarianism or political astuteness. To Second Isaiah, however, the events took on an important faith meaning. It was God who called Cyrus and empowered him to subdue the Babylonians. This was God's way of bringing about the return of the exiles and making possible the rebuilding of the temple of Jerusalem.

> Thus says Yahweh to his anointed, to Cyrus,
> whom he has taken by his right hand
> to subdue nations before him
> and strip the loins of kings,
> to force gateways before him
> that their gates be closed no more:

I will go before you
leveling the heights.
I will shatter the bronze gateways,
smash the iron bars.
I will give you the hidden treasures,
the secret hoards,
that you may know that I am Yahweh,
the God of Israel, who calls you by your name.
It is for the sake of my servant Jacob,
of Israel my chosen one,
that I have called you by your name,
conferring a title though you do not know me.
I am Yahweh, unrivaled;
there is no other God besides me.
Though you do not know me, I arm you
that men may know from the rising to the setting of the sun
that, apart from me, all is nothing (Isaiah 45:1-6; see also
    41:25-29; 48:12-16; Ezra 1:1-4).

Word and Sign in the Gospel

Jesus' ministry centered on the proclamation that the
kingdom of God had come. Jesus pursued this ministry by
teaching and by healing, by word and by sign. The gospels center on key themes of Jesus' preaching, and on some of the redemptive actions of Jesus. Here we need only recall three
examples of how Jesus communicated through word and sign
in his ministry.

In his preaching Jesus proclaimed that he was the way,
the truth and the life (John 14:6). He made claim to an authority that went beyond the Mosaic code. He pointed to a
new way of relationship with God.

This fullness of God's blessing that Jesus came to bring is
symbolized in the changing of the water into wine at the mar-

riage feast of Cana. John notes that the water was in large stone jars provided for the Jewish purification rites. It was this water that Jesus changed into an abundance of the best wine. The Hebrew prophets had described the messianic era as a time when there would be an abundance of wine (see, for example, Amos 9:13-15). As biblical scholars indicate, this action is a sign that points to the messianic nature of Christ's mission. He replaces the purification rites with something better.

John 6 relates another incident where a significant dimension of Jesus' messianic mission is revealed through word and sign. Jesus fed a crowd of five thousand with five barley loaves and two fish. When all had eaten enough, there were twelve hampers of scraps left over. The deeper significance of this sign is explained in Jesus' teaching: "I am the bread of life. He who comes to me will never be hungry; he who believes in me will never thirst" (John 6:35). "I am the living bread which has come down from heaven. Anyone who eats this bread will live forever; and the bread that I shall give is my flesh, for the life of the world" (John 6:51).

One of the central beliefs proclaimed in the gospel is the resurrection. Christ, risen from the dead, will raise us up on the last day. In John 11 Jesus performed a sign manifesting that he is the source of our life and resurrection. Lazarus, his friend, had been buried for four days. Jesus stood outside the tomb and cried out: "Lazarus, here! Come out!" Immediately, Lazarus came out (John 11:43-44).

Summary

To those with faith, God communicates through word and sign. The words explain the sign. The sign visibly manifests the meaning of the word. In the Old Testament God spoke his creative and convenantal love. To those with faith the creation of the world, the deliverance of the Israelites from slavery in Egypt and the return of the exiles were clear signs of God's faithfulness. In the gospels the ministry of Jesus also consisted of word and sign. The claims that Jesus made in his preaching and teaching were symbolized in extraordinary actions. Both the Old and New Testaments enable us to understand how God and Christ continue to transform through word and sign those who have the faith to believe and respond.

REFLECTION/DISCUSSION QUESTIONS

1. Describe three other ways in which the Old Testament depicts God as communicating through word and sign.
2. Illustrate three other examples of how Jesus ministered through word and sign in the gospels.
3. What are some of the ways in which God continues to communicate to us today through word and sign?
4. If God's self-communication through word and sign is to bring about personal transformation in the individual, there must be faith. Explain why this is so.

Chapter 3
Christ, the Sacrament of God's Presence

"At various times in the past and in various different ways, God spoke to our ancestors through the prophets; but in our own time, the last days, he has spoken to us through his Son. . . . He is the radiant light of God's glory and the perfect copy of his nature . . ." (Hebrews 1:1-3). With these words, the author of the letter to the Hebrews gives a succinct summary of the history of God's self-revelation.

The prologue of John's gospel highlights in a similar way this same significance of Jesus.

> In the beginning was the Word:
> the Word was with God
> and the Word was God. . . .
>
> The Word was made flesh,
> he lived among us,
> and we saw his glory,
> the glory that is his as the only Son of the Father,
> full of grace and truth. . . .
>
> Indeed, from his fulness we have, all of us, received—
> yes, grace in return for grace,
> since, though the Law was given through Moses,
> grace and truth have come through Jesus Christ.

> No one has ever seen God;
> it is the only Son, who is nearest to the Father's heart
> who has made him known (John 1:1, 14, 16-18).

Jesus Christ is the fullness of God's self-communication to humans. He is the unique sign among us of God's presence. He is, in the words of Dominican theologian Edward Schillebeeckx, the sacrament of our encounter with God. In this chapter we probe the reality of Christ as the sacrament of God's presence. We do so by reflecting on Jesus as the enfleshment of God's word, on the gospel testimony regarding Jesus of Nazareth, and on the risen Christ as the source of the Spirit.

God's Word Enfleshed

Through the incarnation the word of God became flesh and dwelt among us. In the person of Jesus God's word took on human form. The divine and human came together in complete unity. Jesus became the human and visible manifestation of who God is for us. Because of this extraordinary union God communicates to humans in a unique way through the humanity of Jesus.

By virtue of the reality of the incarnation, Jesus Christ is the basic sacrament of our encounter with God. God is intimately present to humanity in and through the human life of Jesus. Through the person of Christ humans can perceive, experience and approach God in a new way. Even though Jesus is no longer visibly present in mortal flesh on this earth, we can think of him in terms of the humanity we share in common. Despite the fact that we cannot adequately "picture" what risen bodily life is like, we can relate in faith to Jesus Christ as the One who has the fullness of human life in resurrection. Because of our belief that the risen Christ is the word of God, and totally at one with God whom he calls "Abba" ("Father"), to know Christ is to be in touch with God's very word. To experience the presence of Christ is to be in God's presence. Through the action of Christ, God touches us. In, with and through the human Christ we approach God.

The Gospel Testimony

While there is no direct way of knowing the risen Christ, Christians are aided by the witness the gospels give us about Jesus. The gospels themselves were written after two or three generations of Christian reflection on Jesus, in light of his death and resurrection and the experience of the Spirit at Pentecost. Reflection on who this person Jesus of Nazareth was, as perceived through the witness of the gospels, can lead to a better understanding of the risen Christ. Contemplating the mind and heart of the man Jesus can bring about a deeper awareness of the mind and heart of Christ today. A fuller appreciation of the meaning Jesus had for the life of his apostles and disciples can help in the ongoing search for the significance Christ can have for human life in the contemporary world. Through this growing communion with Christ who is the living sign and sacrament of God, Christians are drawn into fuller union with God.

There are countless concrete characteristics of Jesus that enable us to know who Christ is and hence to perceive what kind of God is the "Abba" of Jesus Christ. Only several of these will be noted here.

Love

The first letter of John describes God succinctly: "God is love" (1 John 4:16). The immediate reaction to this statement might be: "What is love?" Jesus deepened and broadened the meaning of love. The Old Testament command was to love one's neighbor. Proportionate retribution (one eye for one eye, one tooth for one tooth) was acceptable. The love that Jesus practiced and preached included one's enemy as well as one's neighbor. It demanded praying for those who hate and persecute us (Matthew 5:44). Jesus' love reached out and embraced the outcasts (the enemies) of Jewish society at the time: the Samaritan, the leper, the prostitute, the tax collector. In this way Jesus manifested the universality of the love of God who "causes his sun to rise on bad men as well as good, and his rain to fall on honest and dishonest men alike" (Matthew 5:45). God's love knows no bounds.

Faithfulness

Jesus' love and commitment to his fellow humans was steadfast. Judas betrayed him. Jesus called Judas "my friend" (Matthew 26:50). Peter denied him. Jesus forgave him. The disciples abandoned him on the night of his arrest. On Easter Jesus reconciled them with his greeting of peace (John 20:20). Jesus' unfailing commitment to humans, even in their blatant infidelity, is a poignant sign of the faithful kindness of God.

Truthfulness

In an extraordinary way Jesus was in touch with himself and his own truth. He unabashedly communicated this truth to all who would hear. Jesus also revealed the truth about the dignity and goodness of humanity. But he did not stop there. He was not afraid to reveal to others their hypocrisy and spiritual bankruptcy, in order to bring them to self-awareness and conversion. (See, for example, Matthew 23.)

Lack of Pretentiousness

There has often been a tendency to impose on God the human trappings and exaltation associated with royalty. This has put God at a great distance from the ordinary human. Jesus' unpretentiousness serves as an important corrective. Jesus was born in a stable and raised among the ordinary folk of Nazareth. He was an itinerant preacher who had no place to lay his head. He spurned titles and worldly honors, and associated with fishermen. Finally, he died penniless, in ill repute, and was buried in a donated tomb.

Compassion

A perennial question that plagues humans is: Where is God in our suffering? Most attempts to address this question leave the impression of a God uninvolved and unperturbed with the vulnerabilities of the human condition. Jesus, as sacrament of God, presents an opposite view. He wept over Jerusalem and at the tomb of his friend Lazarus. He saw a large crowd of people and "took pity on them and healed their sick" (Matthew 14:14). During a funeral procession he was touched at the sight of a widowed mother in Naim. He identified totally with the human plight freely accepting an unjust and tortuous death.

Openness to the Needy

A major theme throughout the gospel is Jesus' availability to the poor, the sick, and the needy. Jesus came to heal the afflicted and to bring new hope to the disadvantaged. He preached that feeding the hungry, giving drink to the thirsty, and visiting the sick and the imprisoned were necessary for entering the kingdom. The healing ministry of Jesus gives evidence of God's concern and involvement with all humans who are in need.

The character of Jesus enables us to perceive God in a truer light. The gospel image of Jesus is incompatible with notions of God as a royal warrior or a heartless judge. To say that Jesus Christ is the sacrament of God is to say that in his humanness is reflected the true nature of God.

Christ: Source of the Spirit

Sacraments are not just signs that tell us about God. They are effective signs, that is, they give grace. We have already seen that grace is not a quantitative commodity, but is relationship with God. Christ is the foundational sacrament of God. He is the source of the Spirit of God. Having died and now risen from the dead, Christ is the font of living waters, the gift of the Spirit (John 7:37-39). This reality is described by John in the post-resurrection appearance of Jesus to the disciples. The doors were closed in the room where the disciples were. Suddenly Jesus came and stood among them and said to them: "Peace be with you." He then breathed on them, saying, "Receive the Holy Spirit" (John 20:20-22).

The giving of the Spirit is an ongoing event. The risen Christ continues to dwell in our midst, giving us the Spirit who enables us to live in relationship with the God whom Jesus calls "Abba" and to live in sisterhood and brotherhood with one another.

Summary

Before there could be any of the seven sacraments, there had to be Christ. Jesus Christ is the primordial sacrament of our encounter with God. Through the incarnation God is present to humanity in an intimate way. Through the person of Jesus Christ, God is revealed to us in a unique manner. By the power of the Spirit given through the crucified and risen Christ we are enabled to enter into new relationship with God as the "Abba" of Jesus Christ, and with one another as sisters and brothers in Christ.

REFLECTION/DISCUSSION QUESTIONS

1. Explain what it means to say that Jesus Christ is the sacrament of our encounter with God.
2. Why is an understanding of Christ as the sacrament of God necessary for understanding the meaning of "the seven sacraments"?
3. In your own personal religious journey how have you experienced Christ as the sacrament of God? In other words, how has your knowledge and love of Christ helped you to know and relate to God?

Chapter 4
The Church:
Sacrament of the Risen Christ

The risen Christ cannot be seen by mortal eyes. He is present to us solely in faith. The only persons we can see are those mortal human beings who are our contemporaries during our sojourn on this planet. The Church on this earth is the sacrament of the risen Christ, because it is composed of mortal, visible human beings who through their faith give witness to Christ's presence. While we cannot directly hear and see Christ, we can visibly and tangibly experience the community of Christians. We can hear their words of faith, and see their lives of Christian discipleship. Through this community Christ is present and communicates to those with faith.

In this chapter we examine how the church, the community of Christ's followers, sacramentalizes Christ through its faith and its discipleship. We then reflect on the relationship between the church and the seven sacraments.

Faith

The notion of faith has too frequently been reduced to intellectual acceptance of the teachings of church authority. While this is a dimension of Christian faith, it is only one aspect of it. Biblically, faith is much more. Christian faith involves personal acceptance of the crucified and risen Christ in our lives. It implies commitment to friendship with Christ. Christian faith accepts the value system of Christ's gospel. It believes in the redemptive value of participating in the death and resurrection of Christ, with all that implies for the individual Christian and for the community.

Through this kind of faith the risen Christ becomes present to Christians in a conscious and explicit way. In faith, Christians are able gradually to put on the mind and heart of Christ. They are able to manifest Christ not only in their proclamation of faith and their worship, but also in their attitudes and in their way of life.

Discipleship

Sometimes there has been far greater concern manifested regarding orthodoxy (correct religious doctrine) and not enough regarding orthopraxis (correct practice of the faith). While verbal proclamations of faith are important, behavior speaks even more loudly what we believe. To be the sacrament of Christ it is indispensable that the Christian community show its discipleship of Christ in a practical living way.

Discipleship involves living out the entire gospel message of Christ. Here, for the sake of example, it is enough to highlight three specific elements.

Love

At the last supper Jesus described the most essential element of discipleship. "By this love you have for one another, everyone will know that you are my disciples" (John 13:35). Later on he states: "A man can have no greater love than to lay down his life for his friend" (John 15:13). The author of 1 John describes further the love that Christians ought to have: "Our love is not to be just words or mere talk, but something real and active" (1 John 3:18).

The church only gives sign of Christ's love for humanity by manifesting love for one another and for the entire human family. This love creates new life to the degree that it involves the gift of self to others. This involves the willingness to put oneself out for another, and to sacrifice certain vested interests out of concern for others.

Embracing the Outcasts

An essential element of Jesus' love was his outreach to the outcasts of his time. He went against the institutionalized prejudices and broke bread with those who were considered sinners. In order to sacramentalize Christ's love for the outcasts, Christians need to examine their own prejudices and attitudes toward today's minority groups. The handicapped, the mentally ill, the divorced, the homosexual are some examples that come to mind.

Priority of Persons over Things

The Christian accepts the basic value system of Christ. While Jesus appreciated things, he relativized their value. People are more important than things. People are even more important than institutions like the sabbath. "The sabbath was made for man, not man for the sabbath" (Mark 2:27). Christian discipleship implies the willingness to sacrifice certain institutional goods for the well-being of individuals.

These are only three examples of the qualities that are involved in the following of Christ. They suffice to make clear the necessity of Christ-like behavior if Christians are truly to sacramentalize Christ to the world.

Church and Sacraments

The church is not only the sacrament of Christ because it gives sign of Christ to the world, but also because Christ is really present in the midst of the community bestowing his grace on it. All that the church becomes as an authentic community of followers of Christ is only possible because of the transforming presence of Christ. All that the Christian community does in response to the action of Christ is sacramental.

Within the context of this sacramentality of the church there are formal ritual actions which we call the sacraments. The presence and action of Christ in the seven sacraments needs to be seen in the context of the ongoing presence and action of Christ in the living community.

The special moments of encounter with Christ known as sacraments correspond to key points in one's journey in life. For most Christians baptism is celebrated shortly after birth. The newborn who has been accepted into the family now receives new birth that comes through Christ, and is initiated into the Christian community. Confirmation and Eucharist are intimately connected with baptism, for together they comprise the rites of full initiation into the Christian community.

One of the major decisions a person must make in life is whether or not to be married. The sacrament of marriage celebrates the decision of two people to weld their lives together in permanent and exclusive commitment.

Another important decision is how a Christian is going to participate in the ongoing ministry of Christ and the church. The sacrament of orders celebrates one's entrance into certain official ministerial roles reserved for the ordained.

Two of the conditions that touch the life of every human are that of sinfulness and mortality. We are born into a world alienated and wounded by hatred, war and exploitation. From the first moments of our life we carry the seeds of bodily mortality within us. We also, of course, enter a human scene that has been redeemed by Christ. Through the sacrament of reconciliation we celebrate with hope the power of Christ to reverse the personal alienations that pull us apart. We especially can do so at those moments when we are most keenly aware of our sinfulness and our need for forgiveness. Through the anointing of the sick we open ourselves to the healing power of Christ manifested through the concern and prayer of the community.

The individual sacraments, then, flow from the ongoing life of the church, the people of God, who live in union with Christ, and who receive from him the gift of his Spirit. In turn, participation in the sacraments, as a sign of our response to Christ's action, enables us to experience with greater awareness and commitment the continuous presence and action of Christ in the totality of our Christian lives.

Summary

The Christian Church is the people of God who express explicit faith in Jesus Christ. As such, the church is the sacrament of the risen Christ on this earth. However, the effectiveness of this sacramentality depends not only on how the good news of Christ is proclaimed to the world in teaching and preaching, but also on how fully Christians allow the Spirit of Christ to penetrate their lives and to inspire their decisions and actions. The seven sacraments flow from the continued union between Christ and his followers. These formal ritual actions celebrate key moments in the ongoing journey of faith in the life of the individual and of the church. It is to the discussion of these individual sacraments that we now turn.

REFLECTION/DISCUSSION QUESTIONS

1. How is the church the sacrament of Christ?
2. What kind of faith do the people who constitute the church need to have in order to sacramentalize the presence of Christ?
3. What modes of behavior in the church actually give sign of Christ to the world? What modes of behavior are counter-signs?
4. What are some of the practical implications the sacramentality of the church ought to have for Christian living today?

Part Two

BAPTISM AND CONFIRMATION

Baptism and confirmation are intrinsically linked as two of the three sacraments of initiation. At one time confirmation was not even perceived as a distinct sacrament. It was a rite performed during the baptismal ceremony.

As the first of the sacraments of initiation, baptism is fundamental to the life of a Christian. It is a sacrament that is received once and for all, and yet it has an ongoing dimension. To be baptized is to be incorporated into a new life with Christ and into a new relationship with the Christian community. In baptism we embark on a journey toward growing union with Christ and with one another. In baptism we are called to share in the redemptive mission that Christ continues to perform in and through the Church. Confirmation, on the other hand, strengthens all of these aspects of the life of a baptized person.

This section probes the important dimensions of the significance that baptism has for the Christian. Since baptism is a participation in the death and resurrection of Christ, we begin by reflecting on Christ's own baptismal experience. The subsequent three chapters probe how through water baptism we receive the gift of the Spirit, share in the death and resurrection of Christ, and participate in the life and mission of the Church. Chapters 9 and 10 treat of important components of the new rite of Christian initiation of adults and the controversial question of infant baptism. In the final chapter we reflect on confirmation and its relationship to baptism.

Chapter 5
The Baptismal Experience of Jesus

In the synoptic account of the public ministry, the baptismal experience of Jesus begins with his baptism at the Jordan and ends with that baptism "with which I must be baptized" (Mark 10:38; see also Luke 12:50), namely his death and resurrection. In the synoptic gospels the baptism at the Jordan and the temptations form a unit, since the latter specify the nature of the messianic ministry to which Jesus commits himself. In this chapter we reflect on the Jordan experience, the temptations in the desert, and the culmination of Jesus' ministry in the baptismal experience of death and resurrection.

The Baptism at the Jordan

Matthew narrates the baptism of Jesus in this way:

Then Jesus appeared: he came from Galilee to the Jordan to be baptized by John. John tried to dissuade him. "It is I who need baptism from you" he said "and yet you come to me!" But Jesus replied, "Leave it like this for the time being; it is fitting that we should, in this way, do all that righteousness demands." At this, John gave in to him.

As soon as Jesus was baptized he came up from the
water, and suddenly the heavens opened and he saw the
Spirit of God descending like a dove and coming down on
him. And a voice spoke from heaven, "This is my Son, the
Beloved; my favor rests on him" (Matthew 3:13-17).

John the Baptist preached a forthright message: "Repent,
for the kingdom of heaven is close at hand" (Matthew 3:2). Accordingly, John insisted on the need for his hearers to turn
from their sins and have a conversion of heart. As a sign of this
repentance and openness to God, people came to John to be
baptized by immersion in the waters of the Jordan.

It is during this period of John's baptizing that Jesus embarked on his public ministry of proclaiming that the kingdom
of God was at hand. Jesus signified his commitment to do the
work God had given him to do, by coming to John to be baptized at the Jordan.

The River Jordan had a lot of significance for the Jews.
After the death of Moses, it was the Jordan River that the Israelites, under the leadership of Joshua, crossed to get to the
promised land. It was at the Jordan River that Elijah passed
on the prophetic mantle to Elisha. It was here at the Jordan
that Jesus, the one perceived by the New Testament writers
as greater than the prophets, gave public manifestation of entering into his ministry which would liberate humanity from
sin and lead humans to a new covenant with God and with one
another.

After the baptism, as Jesus came up from the water, he
saw the Spirit of God come down on him. He also heard a
voice: "This is my Son, the Beloved; my favor rests on him."
These words are based on the servant songs of Isaiah. In these
songs, the servant of Yahweh listens to the word of God and
proclaims it. In the fourth song the servant suffers and is glorified. The gospels see Jesus as the ultimate servant of God.

The voice in the baptism narrative gives witness to this significance of Jesus.

Jesus embarked on his public ministry conscious that the Spirit of God was with him. He embraced his mission that would lead to his sharing in the lot of the suffering servant.

The Temptations

In the synoptic gospels the temptations take place in the wilderness prior to the public ministry. In John's gospel parallels to these temptations occur during Jesus' ministry. One of the levels of meaning of these temptations is that they correspond to three false messianic expectations prevalent at the time of Jesus. Jesus' outright rejection of these temptations make clear his fidelity to the commitment, manifested in his baptism, to fulfill the mission God had given him.

In Matthew's narrative in Chapter 4, the tempter first said to Jesus, "If you are the Son of God, tell these stones to turn into loaves." Quoting from the book of Deuteronomy, Jesus replies: "Man does not live on bread alone but on every word that comes from the mouth of God."

In John's gospel some of the Jews approached Jesus the day after he had fed the five thousand with the loaves and fishes. They were interested in material bread. Jesus replied: "I tell you most solemnly, you are not looking for me because you have seen the signs but because you had all the bread you wanted to eat. Do not work for food that cannot last, but work for food that endures to eternal life, the kind of food the Son of Man is offering you, for on him the Father, God himself, has set his seal" (John 6:26-27).

In both instances Jesus, despite the false expectations of some, refused to reduce his ministry to providing a material utopia. In order to bring humans to new life he must proclaim God's word and lead them to conversion of heart.

In the second temptation in Matthew, the tempter led Jesus to Jerusalem and had him stand on the parapet of the temple. Using Psalm 91 as an argument the tempter challenged: "If you are the Son of God throw yourself down." Jesus' response was again from Deuteronomy: "You must not put the Lord your God to the test."

In John's gospel, some of the people asked Jesus, "What sign will you give to show us that we should believe in you?" (6:30). Jesus performed no sign that would "prove" the faith. There is no such proof. Despite the expectation that some had to the contrary, Christ's messianic ministry was not accompanied by spectaculars that would prove to the unbelieving that what he claimed was true. Christian discipleship is built on faith. Whatever Christ did could only be a sign to those who are willing to believe.

In the final temptation in Matthew, the tempter showed Jesus the splendor of all of the kingdoms of the world. "I will give you all these," he said, "if you fall at my feet and worship me." Once more, quoting from Deuteronomy, Jesus responded, "Be off, Satan! For scripture says: 'You must worship the Lord your God, and serve him alone.'"

This temptation corresponds to the desire that a number of Jews, especially the Zealots, in the early first century had for a messiah-king who would lead the Jews in a political revolution against the Roman empire. After the multiplication of loaves in John's gospel, Jesus could see that some of the people were about to come and take him by force and make him king, and he escaped back to the hills by himself (John 6:15). As Jesus was to say later to Pilate, "Mine is not a kingdom of this world" (John 18:36). Jesus did not come to change the human situation by political power and military might. The human situation can only be redeemed through a conversion of heart.

Jesus' ministry was to proclaim and make present the kingdom (reign) of God. This is a kingdom of truth and love, of peace-making and justice, of compassion and forgiveness. The kingdom Christ preached is a new presence of God that enables humans to relate to God as the "Abba" of Jesus, and to relate to each other as sister and brother.

Death and Resurrection

Throughout his public ministry Jesus was faithful to the commitment signified in the baptism and the temptations. He proclaimed God as his "Abba" (the intimate form of Father, equivalent to our informal "Daddy"), even though some accused him of blasphemy. He preached a new way of life that went beyond the Mosaic law, even though some saw him in violation of the Mosaic tradition. He reached out to the outcasts—lepers, Samaritans, tax collectors, sinners—even though such contact was prohibited to Jews at the time.

His ministry led to rejection by some of the higher religious authorities. Because of the hostility and opposition his ministry generated, Jesus was finally put to death by crucifixion at the hands of the Romans. He was executed as a blasphemer and a political criminal.

Despite all the opposition, and even in the face of death, Jesus remained steadfast in his commitment to pursue the mission God had given him. In his acceptance of death, Jesus manifested in an ultimate way the openness to God that he had signified in the baptism at the Jordan, in the temptations, and throughout his ministry.

Through death Jesus passed into new bodily risen life. Transformed in risen life, Christ is totally filled with the Spirit. At one with the God who is his "Abba," Christ is with his people, giving them his Spirit, and enabling them to die and to be reborn in new union with God and with one another.

Summary

Jesus entered his public ministry by being baptized by John in the Jordan. In this ritual he proclaimed his commitment to God and experienced God's approval. By his rejection of the temptations and by his ministry, Jesus constantly reaffirmed the commitment signified in his baptism. In accepting death, which was the direct result of his mission, Jesus sealed his total openness to do the will of the One who sent him. God vindicated Jesus by raising him up on the third day. In risen life, Christ is at one with God and present to humans in a new way, continuing in the fullest way possible the work of bringing about the kingdom (the reign) of God.

REFLECTION/DISCUSSION QUESTIONS

1. What does the baptism at the Jordan tell us about Jesus and his relationship to God?
2. How do the temptations clarify for us the nature of Jesus' messianic ministry?
3. In what way was the event of Jesus' death and resurrection a baptism?
4. What practical implications does the baptismal experience of Jesus have for living out one's baptismal commitment today?

Chapter 6
Water and the Spirit

Jesus' baptism in the Jordan was a water ritual in which he experienced the gift of the Spirit. The sign in Christian baptism is the immersion or pouring of water. Through this sacramental sign, the newly baptized receives the gift of the Holy Spirit. In this chapter we first examine the meaning of water in the human experience. We then probe what the sign of water tells us about the gift of the Spirit that it effectively signifies. To do this we will reflect on the water theme in the prophets and in John's gospel.

Water

From the beginning of our lives water is an integral part of our human experience. Among the many meanings of water, several can be specified here.

Water is life-giving. We water our plants and our lawns. We yearn for rain so that our harvests will be fruitful and the pastures green. The dry and barren desert stands as a stark sign of the earth's need for water.

Human life is even more directly linked with water. The embryo develops in a sac of amniotic fluid, often referred to as "water." The human body requires quantities of water to stay alive.

Water is thirst-quenching. In fact it is the most basic thirst-quencher. How often after drinking another beverage, we need a drink of water!

Water cleanses and purifies. A warm bath soothes and comforts. A cold shower invigorates. A swim in the pool on a hot day cools and refreshes.

Water fascinates us by its vastness and its power. We stand in awe and wonder as we look over the endless expanse of Lake Michigan, or watch the waterfalls in Niagara, or the waves of the Pacific roll in on a windy day.

Finally, we are only too keenly aware of the uncontrollableness of water and its ability to wreak havoc with our "order" and to inflict sudden death. Water has brought down some of the mightiest of ships. Flood waters have devastated homes and disrupted the lives of entire cities.

Water: A Prophetic Symbol

In the hot desert land of ancient Palestine, water was one of the most valued commodities. It is not surprising, then, that the prophets used water as a symbol for the blessings and richness of life that God would shower on the Jews.

Second Isaiah, prophesying to his fellow Jews during the discouraging and difficult period of the Babylonian exile in the sixth century, B.C.E., offered hope of future salvation.

> The poor and needy ask for water, and there is none,
> their tongue is parched with thirst.
> I, Yahweh, will answer them,
> I, the God of Israel, will not abandon them.
>
> I will make rivers well up on barren heights,
> and fountains in the midst of valleys;
> turn the wilderness into a lake,
> and dry ground into waterspring.

In the wilderness, I will put cedar trees,
acacias, myrtles, olives.
In the desert I will plant juniper,
plane tree and cypress side by side;

so that men may see and know,
may all observe and understand
that the hand of Yahweh has done this,
that the Holy One of Israel has created it (Isaiah 41:17-20).

The prophet struck the same theme in another passage:

For I will pour out water on the thirsty soil,
streams on the dry ground.
I will pour my spirit on your descendants,
my blessing on your children.
They shall grow like grass where there is plenty of water,
like poplars by running streams (Isaiah 44:3-4).

Writing about a century and a half later, the prophet Joel
utilized similar imagery:

And all the river beds of Judah
will run with water.
A fountain will spring from the house of Yahweh
to water the wadi of Acacias (Joel 4:18).

The spiritual fruits of this divine outpouring are spelled
out in descriptive terms in several other prophetic passages:

Once more there will be poured on us
the spirit from above;
then shall the wilderness be fertile land
and fertile land become forest.

In the wilderness justice will come to live
and integrity in the fertile land;
integrity will bring peace,
justice gives lasting security (Isaiah 32:15-17).

I shall pour clean water over you and you will be
cleansed; I shall cleanse you of all your defilement
and all your idols. I shall give you a new heart, and
put a new spirit in you; I shall remove the heart of
stone from your bodies and give you a heart of flesh
instead (Ezekiel 36:25-26).

After this
I will pour out my spirit on all mankind.
Your sons and daughters shall prophesy,
your old men shall dream dreams,
and your young men see visions.
Even on the slaves, men and women,
will I pour out my spirit in those days (Joel 3:1-2).

How does one receive this gift of water, the gift of God's
Spirit? First, by placing one's trust in the Lord:

Blessed is the man who trusts in the Lord,
    whose hope is the Lord.
He is like a tree planted beside the waters
    that stretches out its roots to the stream:
It fears not the heat when it comes,
    its leaves stay green;
In the year of drought it shows no distress,
    but still bears fruit (Jeremiah 17:7-8 NAB).

Second, by thirsting for it. Our response to God is one of longing and yearning, as expressed in the prayer of the psalmist:

As a doe longs for running streams,
so longs my soul for you, my God.

My soul thirsts for God, the God of life;
when shall I go to see the face of God? (Psalm 42:1-2).

Water and the Spirit in John

Reflecting the prophetic imagery, Jesus, in John's gospel, makes generous use of the water symbol in speaking of the gift of the Spirit. Three particular instances deserve mention.

Nicodemus, a Pharisee, came to Jesus by night. Jesus spoke to him of the life that is necessary, in order to enter the kingdom of God.

I tell you most solemnly,
unless a man is born through water and the Spirit,
he cannot enter the kingdom of God:
what is born of the flesh is flesh;
what is born of the Spirit is spirit (John 3:5-6).

In his conversation with the Samaritan woman at the well, Jesus made even clearer the link between water and the life he came to bring. When the woman came to draw water, Jesus broke the silence: "Give me a drink." She was surprised that being a Jew, Jesus would ask her for a drink, since Jews did not associate with Samaritans. Jesus replied: "If you only knew what God is offering and who it is that is saying to you: 'Give me a drink,' you would have been the one to ask, and he would have given you living water." Further in their conversational exchange, Jesus exclaimed: "Whoever drinks this water will get thirsty again; but anyone who drinks the water that I shall give will never be thirsty again: the water that I shall give will turn into a spring inside him, welling up to eternal life" (John 4:5-14).

The water theme recurs again in Chapter 7 of John's gospel. The feast of Tabernacles was an eight day festival in September-October. The Jews gathered in the Jerusalem temple and prayed for early rains in the winter season. On the last and greatest day of the festival, Jesus stood and cried out: "If any man is thirsty, let him come to me! Let the man come and drink who believes in me." Jesus continued: "As scripture says: 'From his breast shall flow fountains of living water.' " In his narrative John goes on to explain that Jesus "was speaking of the Spirit which those who believed in him were to receive; for there was no Spirit as yet because Jesus had not yet been glorified" (John 7:37-39).

For John, the hour of Jesus' death on Good Friday is the "hour of glory." When Jesus died, one of the soldiers pierced Jesus' side with a lance, and from his side there flowed blood and water (John 19:34).

In John's theology the crucified and risen Christ is the One sent by God to give us the gift of the Spirit. Through the waters of baptism, we receive this new and eternal life. And eternal life is this: "to know you, the only true God, and Jesus Christ whom you have sent" (John 17:3).

Summary

The meaning of water in our human experience and the basic role that water plays in life led the prophets and Jesus to see it as a suitable symbol to describe the inner life of the Spirit of God that is essential for our becoming the people of God. It is this gift of the Spirit that is symbolized in the water rite of baptism.

REFLECTION/DISCUSSION QUESTIONS

1. Reflect on as many personal experiences with water as possible. Which of these were pleasant and life-giving? Which were frightening and life-threatening?
2. What are the ways in which water helps you to understand the meaning of baptism?
3. What are the qualities of water that you find helpful in understanding the Spirit of God?
4. Reflect on three of the biblical texts referred to in this chapter. What further light do these texts shed on the life of the Spirit received in baptism?

Chapter 7
Sharing in Christ's Death and Resurrection

The gift of the Spirit offered in baptism enables us to participate in the death and resurrection of Christ. In this chapter we probe what this sharing means.

Pauline Perspective

We owe to Saint Paul the insight that baptism incorporates us into Christ's death and resurrection.

> You have been taught that when we were baptized in Christ Jesus we were baptized in his death; in other words, when we were baptized we went into the tomb with him and joined him in death, so that as Christ was raised from the dead by the Father's glory, we too might live a new life.
>
> If in union with Christ we have imitated his death, we shall also imitate him in his resurrection. We must realize that our former selves have been crucified with him to destroy this sinful body and to free us from the slavery of sin. When a man dies, of course, he has finished with sin.

But we believe that having died with Christ we shall return to life with him: Christ, as we know, having been raised from the dead will never die again. Death has no power over him any more. When he died, he died, once for all, to sin, so his life now is life with God; and in that way, you too must consider yourselves to be dead to sin but alive for God in Christ Jesus (Romans 6:3-11).

Too often in the past, religious teaching has been preoccupied with the negative aspects of baptism. Baptism "took away original sin." Paul's baptismal theology enables us to appreciate the positive dimension. Through baptism we truly take on an identity with the crucified and risen Christ. This meaning is symbolized by the water rite, and is especially brought out in baptism by immersion. The person being baptized is plunged into the water: a sign of death. (If one were to remain there very long, he would surely die.) One emerges from the water refreshed and invigorated.

In baptism we share in the baptismal experience of Jesus which culminated, as we saw in Chapter 5, in death and resurrection. Jesus went down into the depths of human death willingly and out of love. Unlike Adam who broke with God's will, Jesus responded to God by doing the mission he was sent to do. He did not back away from this mission, even when death at the hands of his enemies became imminent. Having gone down into the pit of death and been buried, Jesus rose from the dead in new bodily risen life. With love and forgiveness Jesus suffered an unjust death as a blasphemer and a criminal. He emerged in resurrection, vindicated by God and filled in a new way with the Spirit of God. Having been put to death by those who attempted to put an end to his ministry, Christ rose from the dead as the source of new life for all.

In baptism, we die to the power sin has over us and live under the influence of the power of the Spirit of Christ. We die to alienation from God and enter into a life of friendship with Christ and through him with the God he calls "Abba." In baptism we die to alienation from each other and live in a community of Christian fellowship. Finally, we die to the values and priorities of a sinful, exploitative "world," and live in a new life governed by the values of Christ's gospel.

This death to sin and rising in Christ that takes place in baptism is not an automatic, once and for all event. Baptism initiates us into a new life that we must daily choose to grow in and to nurture. Through baptism we commit ourselves to a lifelong process of dying to the influences of sin and of growing in the life and spirit of Jesus Christ.

Light and Darkness

The theme of light and darkness is important imagery that can help us further understand the baptismal sharing in Christ's death and resurrection. In the prologue of his gospel, John speaks of Christ as being the true light. All who accept him become the children of God (John 1:9-12). The application of this light imagery to Christ is illustrated in Chapter 9, where John sees the miracle of the cure of the man born blind as a sign that Christ is the light of the world (John 9:5). In John's version of the narrative, Jesus spat on the ground, made a paste with his spittle, and put this over the eyes of the blind man. Jesus then instructed the man to go and wash in the pool of Siloam, which word, John points out, means "sent." (This word takes on significance when we recall that in John's gospel, Christ is called the one who is sent by the Father.) The blind man went off and washed himself, and his physical sight was restored. More remarkable, by the end of Chapter 9, the man born blind has come to the light of true faith in Christ.

Worshiping Christ, the man proclaimed his belief in him as the Son of Man.

Many contemporary biblical scholars see this narrative as a baptismal catechesis. The man, born blind, received his physical sight from Christ through anointing and washing in the water. So too, humans, born into a condition of human sinfulness, receive the light through the sacramental anointing and washing of baptism.

The baptismal life of living in the light does not continue automatically. It involves a lifelong process of making decisions inspired by the light rather than by the powers of darkness.

> This is what we have heard from him,
> and the message that we are announcing to you:
> God is light; there is no darkness in him at all.
> If we say that we are in union with God
> while we are living in darkness,
> we are lying because we are not living the truth.
> But if we live our lives in the light,
> as he is in the light,
> we are in union with one another,
> and the blood of Jesus, his Son,
> purifies us from all sin (1 John 1:5-7).

The author of the First Letter of John goes on to explain concretely what this light and darkness is.

> Anyone who claims to be in the light
> but hates his brother
> is still in the dark.
> But anyone who loves his brother is living in the light
> and need not be afraid of stumbling;
> unlike the man who hates his brother and is in the darkness,
> not knowing where he is going,
> because it is too dark to see (1 John 2:9-11).

In 1 John light is the symbol for love, and darkness is the symbol for hatred. Sharing as a baptized person in the death and resurrection of Christ involves dying to the pockets of hatred that lurk in the human heart, and living more deeply in the light of Christ's love. It means dying to self-centeredness, jealousy, pride and vindictiveness, in order to grow in generosity, concern, humility and forgiveness.

There is also a collective dimension of this dying and rising. As a baptized community we are called to be the body of Christ. In order to become increasingly Christ's body, the church needs ongoing conversion. It must daily die to the dark shadows of institutionalized injustice, complacency and stagnancy that threaten every established organization. Through this dying the church can share in the rising of Christ and become more authentically the people of the light committed to justice, ongoing reform, and dynamic, creative responses to the changing needs of a torn world.

Final Death and Resurrection

All the dyings and risings that make up the Christian journey of life on this earth culminate in death to this mortal bodily existence. In Christian faith we believe that this death marks not the end but a new beginning. In light of our treatment of Christ's baptism in Chapter 5, our own final death and resurrection can be seen as the ultimate stage of our own baptism.

For animals, death is merely something that happens. They are passive victims. For humans, death is radically different. While death is ultimately inevitable, humans, endowed as they are with mind and heart, are able to give death meaning. One can choose to die in bitter cynicism and despair, or with faith and trusting love.

Christ redeemed humans, and indeed radically changed the meaning of death by dying out of sacrificial love for others. He died loving and forgiving his enemies, and thus made possible the reconciliation of the human race. He died commending his life to God who raised him up on the third day.

In baptism Christians commit themselves to Christ. They believe that he makes a difference in their lives and their future destiny. The hour of death presents the ultimate challenge. Is there really anything on the other side of the grave? Is there a personal future beyond this life? For the Christian, facing one's own death with hope and trust becomes the ultimate act of faith and commitment to Christ. It is the final way one participates in the dying and rising with Christ that began in baptism. One makes that final leap of faith into the dark, believing that those who die with Christ will rise with him. Through one's own personal death and resurrection, the process of being transformed in Christ that began in baptism is brought to culmination.

Summary

Jesus' ultimate baptism was his own death and resurrection. Through baptism the Christian shares in the death and resurrection of Christ. One dies to sin and is reborn in Christ. Throughout life one grows in Christ by dying to the influence of darkness and hatred and by living in the light of truth and love. One's baptismal life is brought to fulfillment in the acceptance of death as the passage to risen life.

REFLECTION/DISCUSSION QUESTIONS

1. How would you describe in concrete terms the new life with Christ that one enjoys because of baptism?

2. How does dying to the dark side within enable one to grow as a human person, and to live a happier and more meaningful life? How does it make one more like Christ? Explain with specific examples.
3. How can dying and rising with Christ affect the priorities that govern one's life? Give three examples.
4. Explain how death can be the ultimate affirmation of one's baptismal commitment.

Chapter 8
Initiation into the Community

In the not too distant past there was a strong tendency to view baptism in an individualistic way. Not enough emphasis was given to baptism as incorporating persons into the community of Christians. Indeed, we knew that baptism made us members of a church. Too often, however, "church" was perceived as the place we go to get spiritually refueled in order to "keep the commandments and save our souls."

In the past few decades theology has recaptured the biblical insight that through baptism all Christians are called as members of the Christian community to pursue the fullness of holiness and to participate in the mission that Christ continues in the Church. All humans, after all, are called to salvation. Members of the Church are called to involve themselves in a conscious and explicit way in the mission of the church.

This chapter probes what it means to be a member of the body of Christ. It also examines how the baptized Christian is called to share in Christ's prophetic, priestly and kingly mission.

The Body of Christ

In his first letter to the Corinthians (Chapter 12) Paul speaks of the fact that baptism incorporates the Christian into the risen body of Christ. Christ is one, just as the human body is one, in spite of the number of its members and their diversity. The community of baptized Christians, therefore, is the manifestation and extension of Christ's body on this earth. Because the Church is composed of members who participate in the life of the risen Christ, it is truly the body of Christ.

There are two main points in particular that Paul stresses in his analogy of the body. First, while the human body is made up of many parts, it is a single unit, because all of these parts are united to form a whole. No part exists independently from the others. Together, all of the parts constitute an integral body. So too, all the members of the church, "Jews as well as Greeks, slaves as well as citizens," are all united in Christ, because they were all baptized in the one Spirit (v. 13).

Second, the human body cannot be identified with any one of its parts. Each member has its own importance. "If the ear were to say, 'I am not an eye, and so I do not belong to the body,' would that mean that it was not a part of the body? If your body was just one eye, how would you hear anything?" (vv. 16-17). No one part of the body can say to another part, "I do not need you." So too, each member of the church has his or her unique gift and call. No member can say to another, "I have no need of you." Each member is of unique significance.

> Now you together are Christ's body; but each of you is a different part of it. In the Church, God has given the first place to apostles, the second to prophets, the third to teachers; after them, miracles, and after them the gifts of healing; helpers, good leaders, those with many languages. Are all of them apostles, or all of them prophets, or all of them teachers? Do they all have the gift of miracles, or all have the gift of healing? Do all speak strange languages, and all interpret them? (1 Corinthians 12:27-30).

One of the very essential meanings of baptism is that through this sacrament Christians become an integral part of the church, the body of Christ. This community of Christians can be appropriately called the body of Christ for at least two reasons. First, Christians are united and bonded together with Christ and with one another by the power of the Spirit of God. The baptized truly form a community of persons. They are not just a group of isolated individuals. Second, Christians on earth today do for the risen Christ something like what a body does. Through my human body I can be visibly present to others, and can tangibly communicate to them. The risen Christ is invisible to mortal eyes. His presence can be visibly manifest in the world today through the body of the baptized who consciously and explicitly live in Christ and express through word and action their faith and commitment to him. It is especially through the love that Christians extend to one another and to all humans that the love of Christ is evident on this earth.

Through baptism, then, the Christian is called to be a member of the body of Christ. As such, the baptized person is challenged to live in a way that truly gives witness that Christ is risen and in our midst. By coming to know the Christian community, others ought to be able to know what kind of person the risen Christ really is.

A Priestly People

In the New Testament the author of the first letter of Peter refers to the community of the baptized as a priestly people. Addressing the members of the Christian community, he states: "But you are a chosen race, a royal priesthood, a consecrated nation, a people set apart to sing the praises of God who called you out of the darkness into his wonderful light" (1 Peter 2:9).

The Second Vatican Council picks up this biblical theme and corrects the false notion that would identify priesthood with ordained priests. It is true that through the sacrament of orders priests are ordained for certain leadership roles and ministries in the church. This fact, however, cannot be allowed to obscure the priesthood of all the baptized.

Through baptism all Christians are incorporated into Jesus Christ, the one high priest. "The baptized, by regeneration and the anointing of the Holy Spirit, are consecrated into a spiritual house and a holy priesthood" (*Constitution on the Church*, #10). As this Council document on the Church points out, through all the works befitting Christians, the baptized can offer sacrifices and proclaim the power of God. By prayer and praise of God, they present themselves as a living sacrifice. The baptized bear witness to Christ and point to the hope of eternal life.

This same section of the Constitution describes the relationship between the priesthood of the baptized and and ordained priesthood.

> Though they differ from one another in essence and not only in degree, the common priesthood of the faithful and the ministerial or hierarchical priesthood are nonetheless interrelated. Each of them in its own special way is a participation in the one priesthood of Christ. The ministerial priest, by the sacred power he enjoys, molds and rules the priestly people. Acting in the person of Christ, he brings about the Eucharistic Sacrifice, and offers it to God in the name of all the people. For their part, the faithful join in the offering of the Eucharist by virtue of their royal priesthood. They likewise exercise that priesthood by receiving the sacraments, by prayer and thanksgiving, by the witness of a holy life, and by self-denial and active charity.

To be a priest is to be a mediator between God and humans. In Christian faith, Christ is the one and only mediator. In and through Christ God has come to humans. In and through Christ humans go to God. Christian priesthood is a participation in the one priesthood of Christ. All the baptized share in this priesthood by virtue of their baptism. Christians actively participate in the priestly mission of Christ through liturgy and prayer, and through the witness that they give in the day-to-day living out of Christian discipleship.

The Prophetic Mission

The prophet, in the biblical sense, is one who hears the word of God and proclaims it to the people. In the New Testament Jesus is perceived as one who is greater than the prophets. He is not just another in the line of prophets. Being the word of God enfleshed, Jesus gives witness to God in a new and unique way. Because of his extraordinary experience of God, Jesus is able to proclaim that God is his "Abba."

Through baptism Christians participate in the prophetic mission of Christ. In the *Constitution on the Church,* the bishops at the Second Vatican Council speak of this prophetic mission. "The holy people of God shares also in Christ's prophetic office. It spreads abroad a living witness to him, especially by means of a life of faith and charity and by offering to God a sacrifice of praise, the tribute of lips which give honor to his name" (#12).

Christians fulfill their prophetic mission by proclaiming those elements of faith that are unique to Christianity: belief in Christ as the word of God enfleshed and as Savior of all humanity, and hope in the resurrection. The prophetic mission also entails giving witness to the value system inherent in the gospel. This includes the threefold conviction that persons are more important than things, that in Christ all humans—including the social outcasts—are owed love and concern, and that it is by losing one's life that one saves it.

The Kingly Mission

In light of our human experience, we most commonly associate kingship with power—as well as its abuse—and with wealth. To speak of the kingly mission of Jesus is to revolutionize the notion "king." In the gospels the image of Jesus as king is associated with the cross. Attached to the cross was the inscription "Jesus the Nazarene, King of the Jews." On the cross Jesus died in weakness and poverty. The power of Jesus' kingship is the power of sacrificial love. Because he died out of love for humans, the risen Christ has the power to inspire and transform all who are responsive to him.

Through baptism all Christians are called to share in the mission of Christ to proclaim and promote the kingdom (the reign) of God among humans. Even though the kingdom of God will not come to fulfillment until that eschatological moment at the end of time, it is already present to the degree that humans allow God to influence their lives. Baptism challenges Christians to allow God's truth and love to affect the way they conduct themselves in their lives and in their relationships with others.

What it means to proclaim the kingdom (reign) of God is made concrete in Jesus' teaching in the gospel. For our purposes here we can cite five characteristics of God's reign in our lives: love, forgiveness, honesty, compassionate concern and peacemaking. The love that Jesus speaks of must include the enemy as well as the neighbor. Only through our forgiveness of one another is the alienation of sin taken away. We are called to be so trusting and honest with one another that oaths become unnecessary. Membership in the kingdom demands feeding the hungry, giving drink to the thirsty, clothing the naked, and visiting the sick and imprisoned. Finally, God's reign leads us to put aside the sword and to solve our problems by *making* peace.

Summary

Baptism makes the person an integral member of the church, the people of God, the community of Christians. As such, all Christians constitute the body of Christ. They are called to participate actively in Christ's ongoing priestly and prophetic ministry. The baptized, through their words and lives, are challenged to promote the kingdom (reign) of God proclaimed by Christ.

REFLECTION/DISCUSSION QUESTIONS

1. Explain what this statement means: "We are not members of the church primarily to be saved, but to participate explicitly in the mission of Christ."
2. What does it mean to say that the entire community of the baptized are a priestly people?
3. What is your personal experience of the prophetic mission of others in the church? What is your own experience of participating in the prophetic mission of Christ?
4. How can you as a Christian promote the kingdom (reign) of God in the context of your family life, your work, and in the social environment in which you find yourself?

Chapter 9
The Rite of Christian Initiation of Adults

The rite of Christian initiation of adults reflects the contemporary understanding of baptism that is manifested in the documents of Vatican II. The rite also makes clear the meaning of the baptismal vocation. It is appropriate, then, to take a look in this chapter at the new rites of initiation. In our treatment we will focus on the rite of Christian initiation of adults as it is ordinarily performed. This rite consists of three stages: (1) the rite of becoming catechumens; (2) the rite of election or enrollment of names; (3) the celebration of the sacraments of initiation. Here we merely outline some of the key elements in each of these stages and the periods before and after these stages.

The Rite of Becoming Catechumens

This rite is preceded by a period of time called the pre-catechumenate. This is a time of evangelization in which the person who is not yet Christian hears the first preaching of the gospel. A person who has accepted the initial proclamation of the gospel, and has an elementary faith in Christ, can be admitted to the rite of becoming a catechumen. The rite includes the reception of the candidates, the liturgy of the word, and the dismissal.

The candidates, their sponsors and the faithful gather near the entrance of the church. The celebrant greets them and engages in dialogue with them. After the candidates have declared their desire for faith, the celebrant addresses them in these words:

> God enlightens every man who comes into the world. Through the world he has created, he makes known the unseen wonders of his love so that man may learn to give thanks to his Creator.
>
> You have followed his light. Now the way of the Gospel opens before you, inviting you to make a new beginning by acknowledging the living God who speaks his words of truth to men. You are called to walk by the light of Christ and to trust in his wisdom. He asks you to submit yourself to him more and more and to believe in him with all your heart. This is the way of faith on which Christ will lovingly guide you to eternal life. Are you ready to enter on this path today under the leadership of Christ? (RCIA, #76).

To this the candidates respond: "I am."

The celebrant then traces the sign of the cross on the forehead and senses of the candidates, and prays that they may hear the voice of the Lord, see with the light of God, and respond to God's word.

The liturgy of the word in this and all of the initiation rites follows the standard format of scripture readings, responsorial psalm, and prayers for the catechumens. Appropriate texts can be chosen from a large selection.

In dismissing the candidates, the celebrant recalls briefly the joy with which the catechumens were received, and exhorts them to live according to the word they have heard. He concludes: "My dear catechumens: go in peace. May the Lord be with you always." The catechumens respond: "Thanks be to God."

The catechumenate or pastoral formation of catechumens continues until they have matured sufficiently in their conversion and growth of faith. If necessary, it may last several years. During this period the catechumens learn about the entire Christian faith, are initiated in living the Gospel, and participate in celebrations of the word that are specially designed for them.

The Rite of Election

On the first Sunday of Lent the election or enrollment of names is celebrated. In this rite the catechumens express their intent to receive the sacraments of initiation, and are given formal approval to do so at the Easter Vigil. The rite of election represents the end of the catechumenate and the beginning of the proximate preparation for sacramental initiation. This preparation period extends throughout the season of Lent.

The rite of election takes place after the liturgy of the word and the homily. The person responsible for the initiation of the catechumens presents the elect in these words:

> As Easter draws near, these catechumens are completing their period of preparation. They have been strengthened by God's grace and supported by this community's example and prayers. Now they request that, after further preparation and the celebration of the scrutinies, they will be allowed to receive the sacraments of baptism, confirmation, and the eucharist (#143).

One by one, the elect are called by name and come forward with their godparents. The celebrant questions the godparents about the readiness of the candidates to be numbered among those chosen to receive the sacraments of initiation at the Easter Vigil. Satisfied with the godparents' testimony, the celebrant makes this response.

My brothers and sisters:

These catechumens have asked to be admitted into the sacramental life of the Church at Easter. Those who know them judge them to be sincere in their desire. For a long time they have heard the word of Christ and have attempted to shape their conduct accordingly. They have shared in the fellowship and the prayer of their brothers and sisters. Now I wish to inform all here present of our community's decision to call them to the sacraments. Therefore, I ask their godparents to state their opinion once again, so that all may hear (#145).

After the godparents have given an affirmative answer, the candidates then express their desire to receive baptism, confirmation, and the Eucharist. The names of each are enrolled. The rite ends with prayers for the elect.

The Period of Purification and Enlightenment

For the elect Lent is a period of purification and enlightenment or illumination. During this time the elect give themselves to spiritual recollection so as to prepare for Easter and for the sacraments of initiation. For this purpose the scrutinies, the presentations and the preparatory rites take place throughout the season of Lent. By these rites the spiritual and catechetical preparation of the elect is completed.

The purpose of the scrutinies is to purify the minds and hearts of the elect, to strengthen them against temptation, to purify their intentions, and to make firm their decision. The scrutinies take place in the Masses of the scrutinies on the third, fourth and fifth Sundays of Lent. The first Mass of the scrutinies is always that of the Samaritan woman, the second of the man born blind, and the third of Lazarus. Through the themes of these Masses the elect grow in their understanding of Christ the Redeemer as the source of living water, the light of the world, and our resurrection and life.

Each of the scrutinies takes place in a similar manner. After the homily the elect and their godparents come forward. Prayers are said for the elect. This is followed by the rite of exorcism. In the rite of exorcism "the Church teaches the elect about the mystery of Christ who frees from sin. By exorcism they are freed from the effects of sin and from the influence of the devil, and they are strengthened in their spiritual journey and open their hearts to receive the gifts of the Savior" (#156).

After the exorcism an appropriate song may be sung. This is followed by the dismissal of the elect.

In the rites of presentation, the candidates chosen for baptism receive two documents: the profession of faith, and the Lord's Prayer. The presentation of the profession of faith or creed ordinarily takes place during the week after the first scrutiny. The Lord's Prayer is given to the elect during the week after the third scrutiny. Each rite consists of the liturgy of the word and homily, the presentation of the document and the recitation of the creed or the Lord's Prayer, and a prayer over the elect.

The preparatory rites take place earlier in the day on Holy Saturday so that the elect may dispose themselves by recollection and prayer to receive the sacraments at the Easter Vigil. There are four preparatory rites. The first is the recitation of the profession of faith. This consists of an appropriate song, a scripture reading, a brief homily, a prayer over the elect, and the recitation of either the Apostles' Creed or the Nicene Creed.

The second is the rite of Ephphatha or opening of ears and mouth. By its symbolism, this rite shows the need of grace in order to be able to hear the word of God and respond to it. The celebrant touches with his thumb the ears and mouth of each of the elect, saying: "Ephphatha, that is, be opened, that you may profess the faith you have heard, to the praise and glory of God."

In the next rite the elect indicate their choice of Christian name. This is followed by the anointing of the elect with the oil of catechumens.

Celebration of the Sacraments of Initiation

During the Easter Vigil, after the liturgy of the word, the elect receive the sacrament of baptism. First, the litany of saints is sung. This is followed by the blessing of the baptismal water, the renunciation of sin and evil, and the profession of faith. At this point in the ceremony the elect are baptized by immersion or the pouring of water.

The conferral of the sacrament of baptism is followed by what are called explanatory rites. As their name suggests, these three rites bring out through their symbolism some of the further meaning of baptism.

The first of these explanatory rites is the anointing after baptism. This rite is omitted whenever confirmation immediately follows baptism. This is ordinarily the case in the new rites of Christian initiation. Where the anointing with chrism does take place, the celebrant recites this prayer.

God, the Father of our Lord Jesus Christ,
has freed you from all sin,
given you a new birth by water and the Holy Spirit
and welcomed you into his holy people.
He now anoints you with the chrism of salvation.
As Christ was anointed Priest, Prophet, and King,
so may you live always as a member of his body,
sharing everlasting life (#224).

The second explanatory rite takes place with the godparents clothing the newly baptized with a white garment. As they do the celebrant says:

You have become a new creation
and have clothed yourselves in Christ.
Take this white garment
and bring it unstained to the judgment seat of our Lord Jesus
    Christ
so that you may have everlasting life (#225).

In the final explanatory rite, the godparents light a candle from the Easter candle and hand it to the newly baptized, while the celebrant says these words:

You have been enlightened by Christ.
Walk always as children of the light
and keep the flame of faith alive in your hearts.
When the Lord comes, may you go out to meet him
with all the saints in the heavenly kingdom (#226).

Immediately following these rites, the celebrant confers the sacrament of confirmation. The newly baptized and confirmed then participate in the celebration of the Eucharist.

The Period of Postbaptismal Catechesis or Mystagogia

The rites of Christian initiation are a new beginning, not an end. Hence the rites call for a period of time in which there is special continued involvement between the neophytes and their godparents, pastors, and the community of the faithful. This takes place throughout the Easter season. This is meant to be a time when great care is taken that the neophytes become fully and happily inserted into the life of the community.

On the Sundays during the Easter season, the neophytes take part in the Mass with their godparents. It is recommended that they be mentioned in the homily and in the general intercessions. Around the time of Pentecost, a special celebration closes this period of postbaptismal catechesis.

Summary

The revised rite of Christian initiation of adults shows that Christian life is a process. The precatechumenate period leads up to the rite of becoming a catechumen The catechumenate lasts for months and perhaps years. The end of the catechumenate period is celebrated by the rite of election. This begins the period of purification and enlightenment that takes place during Lent, and serves as an immediate preparation for the sacraments of initiation. These sacraments, conferred at the Easter Vigil, are followed by a period of postbaptismal catechesis.

REFLECTION/DISCUSSION QUESTIONS

1. Explain the meaning of each of the three stages of the rite of Christian initiation of adults.

2. What is the purpose of each of the four periods involved in Christian initiation: precatechumenate, catechumenate, purification and enlightenment, and the postbaptismal catechesis?
3. What does this rite of Christian initiation tell us about the meaning of Christian discipleship?
4. Based on the rite of Christian initiation for adults, design a Christian renewal program for teenagers or adults who were baptized as infants.

Chapter 10
Infant Baptism

The careful screening process and lengthy formation involved in preparing adults for making the free choice to enter the Christian community may well deepen the questions many have already raised concerning infant baptism. Before ending our treatment of baptism we do well to examine this important pastoral issue. First, we will look at the reasons that have been raised against and for the practice of infant baptism. We will then examine several ways in which the celebration of infant baptism could more fully enrich the faith life of the community.

Infant Baptism: A Sound Practice?

Serious questioning of infant baptism is not merely a modern phenomenon. In the early stages of the Reformation, in the first quarter of the sixteenth century, Anabaptists refused to recognize the validity of infant baptism. They demanded that believers be baptized as adults, even if they had received baptism as infants.

Today two basic reasons are raised in opposition to infant baptism. First, it is stated that infant baptism infringes on the freedom of the child. The infant is given no choice in regard to the significant reality of being baptized or not. The second objection raised is that commitment to Christ and to the Christian community signified in baptism involves personal decision. An infant is incapable of such a decision.

In response to these objections, certain points can be raised that serve as a justification for infant baptism. In regard to the first objection, it can be asked whether admitting the child into the Christian community is any more an "infringement" on personal freedom than bringing the child into the world as an American citizen, and as a member of a particular socio-economic group. If we wait until a child is old enough to make an individual choice before we teach the child how to walk, or before we create an environment of love and of educational opportunity in the home, we will actually be limiting the future range of possible choices. To refuse to share as fully as possible one's Christian heritage with the newborn can actually handicap the future free choice that this person will eventually have to make in regard to Christ and to membership in a particular Christian community.

In regard to the second objection, there is no disagreement about the fact that an infant cannot make a free commitment to Christ and the church. However, the real question is whether or not Christ and the church can celebrate their free commitment to the infant. In faith we believe that from the first moment of human existence each person is special to God. The sacrament of baptism can celebrate Christ's self-gift to this child. It can celebrate the love of the parents and their commitment to share their Christian life with this child. Through baptism the Christian community manifests in a sacramental way its acceptance of this child as a member. It makes a commitment to create an environment of Christian faith, love and discipleship that will facilitate the child's growth in Christ. Providing this gift for the infant does not substitute for the personal commitment the child will later have to make. It will, however, plant the seeds for making such a commitment possible.

Pastoral Suggestions

It is not enough merely to give verbal support for the practice of infant baptism. It is also necessary to continue to find ways in which the baptism of an infant can have maximum effect on the faith life of the parents and the Christian community. The following suggestions serve only as a start, and are in no way exhaustive.

1. Welcoming the newborn into the Christian community does not begin with baptism, but with acceptance of the child in the early stages of pregnancy. As psychologists insist, the fetus in the womb is already affected by the love of the parents. If there are siblings, the period of pregnancy is an excellent time to prepare them for accepting the newborn. The return from the hospital can be marked by a family party. These human celebrations of welcome of a new family member culminate in the sacramental expression of our commitment to the child through baptism.

2. Parents can utilize the baptism of a child as an opportunity to enrich their own ongoing religious formation. In preparation for the baptism the parents can reflect on the meaning their own baptism has for their lives. Parents might also profit by attending a good parish baptismal preparation program or by reading a contemporary book on baptism or on the Christian life. They might even find value in making a day of recollection together, perhaps toward the end of the pregnancy.

3. The selection of godparents needs to be made on the basis of Christian commitment and the ability to support the

parents in the ongoing Christian formation of the child. It is inadequate to choose someone to be a godparent merely as a way to pay back a social debt or to honor someone.

4. Parents can become directly involved in the planning of the baptismal liturgy. There are options in regard to the songs, readings, prayers, and certain liturgical formulas. Rather than leave these selections to the celebrant, the parents can together choose what they think is most fitting. Parents and godparents might also do some of the readings. Perhaps a special printed program outlining the ceremony may be made available to the gathered community.

5. It is very fitting that the sacrament of baptism be celebrated in the context of the Eucharist. One option is to perform the baptism during one of the regularly scheduled Sunday Masses. This can work out well in some smaller parishes and where there is a sense of genuine community. It is not advisable if the particular congregation is mostly made up of people who are "fulfilling their obligation" and who are likely to look upon a baptism as an added delay to their rush to the parking lot. A second option is to find a priest to celebrate a special Sunday Mass to which interested members of the community can be invited. Another option is to have a baptismal Mass on a weekday evening.

6. The clothing ceremony takes on more meaning if the white garment given the baptized is a personalized stole. The stole can be made long enough so that it can be worn when the infant grows up and is confirmed and receives First Communion. The person's name and the date of baptism can be embroidered on the stole. Later, the dates of confirmation and First Communion can also be embroidered. The stole can then become a symbol that recalls the link between these three sacraments of initiation.

Summary

Despite the serious objections against infant baptism, there is value and significance in the practice. Baptism sacramentalizes God's gift of himself through Christ to the infant. It also sacramentalizes the community's acceptance and commitment to the newborn. With some careful preparation and creative imagination, parents and the community can make an infant's baptism an occasion for their own ongoing conversion.

REFLECTION/DISCUSSION QUESTIONS

1. What are your own personal attitudes toward infant baptism? If you were baptized as an infant, how do you *feel* about that fact? What are your plans regarding the baptism of future children you might have?
2. Outline what you believe are important ways in which parents can prepare for the baptism of their child.
3. Going beyond the author's suggestions, what do you think are some other ways in which the baptism ceremony can be enhanced?
4. Suggest some practical ways in which the religious formation of a child (and an adult) can be directly related to one's baptism.

Chapter 11
Confirming Baptismal Life

In a previous chapter we already saw that the anointing in confirmation was originally a distinguishable rite that was performed during the baptismal ceremony. Historically, this rite became dissociated from baptism. Today, the rite of Christian initiation of adults reestablishes the unity between these two sacraments. However, since most Catholics are baptized as infants, the majority still receive confirmation many years after their baptism.

In this chapter we first reflect on the giving of the Spirit to the first disciples and apostles. We then examine the sacrament of confirmation and the rite in which it is conferred. Finally we address the question about the age at which this sacrament is received.

The Pentecost Experience

The New Testament makes clear that the birth of the church, the Christian community, took place through the death and resurrection of Christ and the giving of the Holy Spirit. The gospel of John and the Acts of the Apostles provide complementary accounts of the apostles' experience of the giving of the Spirit.

John highlights the fact that the crucified and risen Christ is the source of the Spirit. In his passion narrative John links together the death, the resurrection and the gift of the Spirit. The hour of death is the "hour of glory." John describes Jesus' death this way: "Bowing his head he gave up his spirit" (John 19:30). According to biblical scholars there is an intended double meaning here. The obvious first meaning is that Jesus gave up his spirit, that is, he expired, he died. In light of Johannine theology, however, a further meaning seems intended. Through his death, his hour of glory, Jesus gives us the gift of his Spirit.

Likewise John links the giving of the Spirit with Easter. In the Johannine account, already on Easter Sunday evening the risen Christ appeared to his disciples and breathed the Spirit upon them (John 20:22).

In the Acts of the Apostles Luke describes the giving of the Spirit on the fiftieth day after Easter. They had all gathered in one room when all of a sudden they heard what sounded like a powerful wind from heaven. The noise of it filled the entire house. Something appeared to them that seemed like tongues of fire. These separated and came to rest on the head of each of them. Filled with the Spirit they began to speak foreign languages as the Spirit gave them the gift of speech (Acts 2:1–4).

In describing this experience of the Spirit Luke uses two images that are familiar from Old Testament theophanies. The first is a mighty wind. In the fourth gospel Jesus is recorded as using a similar image. "The wind blows wherever it pleases; you hear its sound, but you cannot tell where it comes from or where it is going. That is how it is with all who are born of the Spirit" (John 3:8). To allow the Spirit to enter one's life is to listen to the Spirit. It is to allow the Spirit to lead, guide and inspire one. In faith and trust one yields to the Spirit, allowing the Spirit to influence one's decisions.

The second image is fire. Fire gives light and heat. The Spirit is the Spirit of truth. In the last supper discourse Jesus spoke of the Spirit of truth "whom the Father will send in my name" and who "will be with you for ever" and "will teach you everything" (John 14:16. 17. 26). The Spirit is also the Spirit of love who enkindles and transforms the human heart.

The power of the Pentecost experience can be seen in terms of the dramatic changes that took place in the apostles. During the public ministry of Jesus they often lacked understanding. They argued with each other about who was more important. They fled when he was arrested. After the Pentecost experience they came to a new understanding of Jesus. They saw how he had to suffer and die in order to enter into his glory. They set aside their vested interests and accepted the role of suffering in their own following of Christ. With courage they went forth to proclaim the good news.

The Sacrament of Confirmation

As seen earlier in this section, baptism is the first of the three sacraments of initiation. Through baptism one receives the gift of the Spirit empowering one to live in union with Christ, and to be a member of the Christian community. Baptism begins a process, a journey toward greater union with Christ and toward fuller participation in the life of the community. In a special way, the sacrament of confirmation strengthens, intensifies, confirms what has taken place in baptism. Through confirmation the gifts of the Spirit are received in a fuller way. The confirmed person is brought more fully into membership in the community. Those who receive confirmation after achieving the use of reason can confirm through this sacrament their response to Christ and their desire to be members of the Christian community.

One of the ways of coming to a more specific understanding of the meaning of confirmation and its relationship to baptism is to reflect on the rite itself. Ordinarily confirmation is conferred within the celebration of the Eucharist. After the reading of the gospel and the homily the candidates renew their baptismal promises and make their profession of faith.

There follows the laying on of hands. This is the biblical gesture by which the gift of the Holy Spirit is invoked. In the rite of confirmation the bishop says this prayer:

> My dear friends:
> in baptism God our Father gave the new birth of eternal life
> to his chosen sons and daughters.
> Let us pray to our Father
> that he will pour out the Holy Spirit
> to strengthen his sons and daughters with his gifts
> and anoint them to be more like Christ the Son of God (#24).

This prayer recalls the baptism of the candidates and so connects the confirmation rite with it.

The bishop and assisting priests then extend their hands over all the candidates as the bishop prays these words:

> All-powerful God, Father of our Lord Jesus Christ
> by water and the Holy Spirit
> you freed your sons and daughters from sin
> and gave them new life.
> Send your Holy Spirit upon them
> to be their Helper and Guide.
> Give them the spirit of wisdom and understanding,
> the spirit of right judgment and courage,
> the spirit of knowledge and reverence.
> Fill them with the spirit of wonder and awe in your presence
>   (#25).

This prayer brings out the continuity of the giving of the Spirit. The Spirit has already freed the candidates from sin and given them new life. Now further gifts of the Spirit are requested. The prayer goes on to specify some of these particular gifts.

The laying on of hands is followed by the anointing with chrism. Chrism is a mixture of oil and balsam or perfume. The bishop dips his right thumb in the chrism and makes the sign of the cross on the forehead of each person to be confirmed. Doing so, he mentions the person by name and says, "Be sealed with the Gift of the Holy Spirit." The anointing with chrism and the accompanying words indicate the effects of the sacrament of confirmation. Signed with the perfumed oil, the baptized person receives the seal of the Lord and the gift of the Spirit.

The confirmation ceremony is followed by the general intercessions which conclude with this prayer:

> God our Father,
> you sent your Holy Spirit upon the apostles,
> and through them and their successors
> you give the Spirit to your people.
> May his work begun at Pentecost
> continue to grow in the hearts of all who believe.
> We ask this through Christ our Lord (#30).

In this prayer the gift of the Spirit in confirmation is linked with the first Pentecost.

The celebration of the Eucharist then continues. At the final blessing at the end of Mass the bishop may use this prayer over the people.

> God our Father,
> complete the work you have begun
> and keep the gifts of your Holy Spirit
> active in the hearts of your people.

Make them ready to live his Gospel
and eager to do his will.
May they never be ashamed
to proclaim to all the world Christ crucified
living and reigning for ever and ever (#33).

This final prayer signals the mission aspect of the vocation of
the confirmed.

Age

The practice regarding the age at which confirmation is
received has varied in different traditions and at diverse periods of history. Basically there are two approaches. One approach is to keep the three sacraments of initiation united in
their proper sequence. In this approach, baptism, confirmation and First Eucharist are conferred at the same time. In
some traditions this practice is maintained whether the recipient is an adult or an infant. The second approach to confirmation is to postpone it until the person is old enough to make
a mature decision to participate more fully in the life and mission of the community.

In the Latin rite of the Catholic Church the present practice in regard to adults is to confer the three sacraments together. In the case of those who are baptized as infants or as
small children, First Communion is received around age
seven, and confirmation is postponed ordinarily to the early or
late teens.

Each of the two approaches have an advantage and a disadvantage. The first approach is the more ancient tradition and
preserves the unity and order of the three sacraments that constitute full initiation into the Christian community. On the
other hand, when it comes to infants, many would object that

at least confirmation and First Communion ought to involve free choice on the part of the recipient. The arguments for and against infant baptism can be raised in favor of or in opposition to infant confirmation and infant Eucharist.

The second approach to confirmation has the advantage of making this sacrament an opportunity for baptized persons to reaffirm consciously their choice for Christ. The disadvantage is that this approach breaks up the unity and proper order of the sacraments of initiation.

Summary

The giving of the Spirit at Pentecost transformed the apostles and enabled them to proclaim the gospel of Christ even at the expense of their own life. The sacrament of confirmation strengthens the Christian in the life of the Spirit received in baptism. It also enables the person to participate in a fuller way in the life and mission of the church. The laying of hands, the anointing with chrism, and the various prayers recited during the rite of confirmation bring out the specific meaning and purpose of this sacrament.

REFLECTION/DISCUSSION QUESTIONS

1. How do John's version of the giving of the Spirit and that in Acts complement each other?
2. What difference did Pentecost make in the lives of the apostles?
3. Reflect on some dramatic ways in which the power of the Spirit has affected your life or the life of someone you know.
4. If you are already confirmed, what impact has that event had on your life? If you have a family would you encourage your children to be confirmed? Why or why not?

Part Three

EUCHARIST

The Eucharist is the last of the three sacraments of initiation. The baptized and confirmed person celebrates full entrance into the Christian community by coming to the one table and partaking of the Lord's supper. In the eating of the bread and the drinking of the cup the Christian proclaims oneness with the body of Christ.

The Eucharist is also the center of Christian living. It expresses all that Christ is for humans. The Eucharist is also an intimate symbol of our response to Christ.

In the first three chapters of this section we probe the meaning of the Eucharist as a meal sacrifice. In doing so we first explore the different dimensions of the human meal experience, and reflect on the meal ministry of Jesus. The two subsequent chapters will treat of the Eucharist as a memorial of Christ's death and resurrection and the real presence of Christ. In Chapters 17 and 18 we explore the relationship of the Eucharist to the various human hungers in the world and the relationship of the Eucharist to the other sacraments. The last chapter in the section reflects on the Eucharistic dimension of authentic Christian spirituality.

Chapter 12
The Human Meal

The Eucharist is a meal sacrifice. As such it is a sacramental sign of Christ's offering of himself to God and to us. An understanding and an appreciation of the Eucharist first depends on our human experience of meals. Many people today complain about how boring Sunday Mass is and how little they get out of it. Part of the reason for such boredom is the lack of reflective experience of the deeper dimensions of a human meal. If one does not experience a sense of community sharing at a meal, why expect to experience it at the Eucharist?

This chapter probes the meaning of a human meal. What are the important elements that constitute truly human eating? In addressing this question we examine the physical, psychological, community and religious dimensions of the human meal.

Physical Nutrition

The first and most obvious meaning of the human meal is that it provides physical nourishment. Humans share with all the animal kingdom the absolute need for food and drink in order to survive, as well as to grow in a healthy and balanced way.

Even on this basic level of physical nourishment, the difference between humans and animals emerges. While animals
are driven by blind instincts, humans intellectually understand their needs. Humans not only know the necessity of food
and drink for survival, but also can appreciate the relationship
of various kinds of food to the diverse needs the body has. Humans can make free choices in regard to their diet that have
an important bearing on weight, the prevention and cure of
diseases, the building of better health, and the possibility for
greater longevity. To some degree our health, well-being, and
length of life on this earth are in our hands. What we decide
to do in regard to food and drink has direct and sometimes lasting effects on us and our lives.

Besides being concerned about one's own physical hunger and thirst, and that of one's family, one can plan to provide
for those without sufficient food and drink. If humans so
choose, they can provide balanced meals and nutritional education for the needy in the neighborhood, the city, and
throughout the world. They can also provide people with the
opportunity to acquire the skills necessary to produce their
own food, and suitable jobs whereby to earn a livelihood. Starvation in a world filled with human minds and hearts is a totally
unnecessary scandal. The skills that have enabled humans to
walk on the moon could certainly provide sufficient food and
drink for the world's population. All that is needed is the commitment and the concern.

Psychological Aspects

Everything that humans do, even the most ordinary actions common to all animals, is transformed by the fact that we
are created rational and loving beings. So it is with the human
experience of eating. We attend not only to the fact of whether

or not there is sufficient food, and how it tastes and smells. We are also affected by the way the food looks, how it is arranged and by the manner in which it is served.

Even more significant to humans is whether or not we have other persons with whom we can share the eating experience. Most people do not prefer to eat alone on a regular basis. We have a need for companionship. We have a desire for someone with whom we can break bread. (In fact the very word "companionship" is from the Latin "com" plus "panis" which means bread.) Through the sharing of our food and drink we converse with one another and share our ideas and feelings. Eating and drinking together helps us communicate our deeper selves. Being personally present to each other in and through the meal transforms the eating experience and gives it the power to bind people together.

Shared meals, then, feed not only the body, but also one's emotional and psychological needs. Through eating and drinking together, people strive to satisfy the yearning they have for acceptance and intimacy.

Community Aspects

A community is distinguished from a mere group of people who happen to be side by side. Community takes place when a number of persons come together because of some common identity and a shared interest in working together to achieve some goal. A family, a professional organization, a girl scout troop, a football team are some examples of community. On the other hand, persons are a mere group when they happen to be in the same place at the same time. People who are lined up at the checkout counter or bumping elbows on a bus may be individually pursuing similar goals, but there is no joint effort.

Community is not a static given. Rather it is something that is always in process. It ever needs to grow. What makes community grow is personal communication.

An important aspect of being community and enhancing communication is coming together at least occasionally to "break bread." One of the high points of most annual conventions, whether they be of teachers, doctors, artisans, or members of a union, is the banquet. Athletic teams, activity clubs, and alumni organizations gather periodically to celebrate with food and drink their association. Religious communities of sisters, priests or brothers have traditionally insisted on the communal meal as both a sign and a means of deepening their shared life.

The most basic human unit is the family. It is unique because it is based on the sexual expression of love and on blood relationship. However, even families do not automatically become intimate communities. In order for family members to become a closely knit community of good friends, they must be present to each other and practice the art of communication. The family meal holds a special place in this ongoing process of intimacy.

Family gatherings and special holidays include a festive meal. Certain family traditions grow up around these occasions. The family dinner is the centerpiece of days like Thanksgiving, Christmas, and Easter. Receptions or parties with special food and drink are an essential part of celebrating weddings, graduations, and anniversaries of family members. The birthday cake, decorated and bedecked with candles, is a highly symbolic way of expressing our gratitude and love for the life of another.

The bonding that takes place at these special meal celebrations is dependent on the amount of bonding that takes place daily in our family relationships, and in our more ordinary meals. While it is impossible for the average family in our contemporary culture to be together for all meals, it is important for growth in intimacy that on some kind of regular basis family members living at home gather around the table to share food and drink as a sign of the deeper sharing of themselves. The degree of sharing of oneself at a family meal is dependent on the quality of sharing that goes on in the total family living. At the same time being really present to one another at table can enhance the bonding that takes place at other moments in our lives together.

Religious Aspects

For people who have faith in God, all of life can be seen and experienced in the context of their belief in God's love and concern. Even the most ordinary action of eating is seen in the light of one's faith experience of God. Food and drink are no longer perceived as merely the work of human hands. They are also seen as ultimately provided by a God who loves and is concerned that all humans be abundantly nurtured. Hence, people of faith approach their meals with thanksgiving, with acknowledgement of God's blessings, and with concern in their hearts that all God's people receive their "daily bread." For the Christian the gifts of the table, like all of God's blessings, come through Jesus Christ, and hence take on a Christic dimension.

For those with committed faith, gathering at table with family members and friends also has a religious aspect. In the biblical tradition human persons are made to the image and likeness of God. Accordingly, as we saw in the first section of the book, human friendship is sacramental of the love of God and the love of Christ. God's love is perceived in the love that others have for us. What we do to others we do to Christ (Matthew 25:40). Where two or three are gathered together in his name, Christ is there in the midst of them (Matthew 18:20).

Another aspect of the religious dimension of the shared meal is the sacrifice involved. Providing a meal involves love and concern. People must put themselves out for others. Someone must do the planning, shop, and pay the bills. Skill, work, and interest go into cooking and serving the meal. Those at table look after one another's needs. They make the effort to be present in a personal way to each other. Finally, they take responsibility for cleaning up after the meal and putting things away. All of this implies a price as well as a satisfaction. In this sense every shared meal is sacrificial in the root meaning of the word (the Latin "sacer" = sacred; "facere" = to make). What makes a meal sacred and of lasting value is the love, effort and concern that people show for one another.

Summary

Eating food and partaking in drink are basic physical functions. For the human these actions take on many deeper levels of meaning. In the shared meal people can satisfy their profound human hunger for understanding, love, and companionship. By coming together to break bread and to share the cup, people form community with one another, and strengthen the bonds between themselves. For a person of faith the shared meal becomes an important sign of God's generosity and a means of experiencing God's love manifested in others.

The best foundation for understanding the sacramental meaning of Eucharist is to appreciate and experience the love and bonding that takes place in shared meals with our family and friends. In this way we can come to experience increasingly the Eucharistic meal as a unique sign of Christ's sacrificial gift of himself in love, and as a significant means for binding ourselves together as a Christian community.

REFLECTION/DISCUSSION QUESTIONS

1. Recall two or three of the most memorable meals you have experienced in your life. Identify the specific reasons why these meals stand out in your mind.
2. What do you see as the importance of the family meal? What are some important guidelines that need to be followed if the family meal is to have a truly bonding effect?
3. How can prayer be integrated into our shared meals? In what ways can food and drink enhance our gatherings for shared prayer?

Chapter 13
The Meal Ministry of Jesus

As in all human lives, meals constituted an important part of the life of Jesus. He needed to eat in order to survive. Sharing food and drink was integrally bound up with his social life. Further, his redemptive concern for humans and his unique mission to them gave an even deeper dimension of meaning to his eating and drinking with others.

In this chapter we reflect on some of the principal meal situations recorded in the gospels. Exploring what Jesus was doing for people in these meals can deepen our insight into what Christ is doing for us in Eucharist.

Eating with Tax Collectors

A theme that recurs often in the gospels is Jesus' eating with tax collectors and sinners. Jewish tax collectors were hated because they collected Roman taxes and extorted them to the limit. The Jews considered them not only oppressors, but also traitors because they collaborated with the Roman empire. The term "sinners" refers to Jews who did not observe the law. Pharisaic Judaism strictly forbade contact with Gentiles and non-observant Jews. In light of this prohibition Jesus' practice of eating with "sinners" is all the more significant.

A narrative in the synoptic gospels reveals the basic principle that led Jesus to violate this prohibition. After Jesus called Matthew, a tax collector, to be one of the Twelve, Matthew invited Jesus to a big dinner. A great number of tax collectors and sinners were at table with Jesus. When the Pharisees saw this, they questioned Jesus' disciples: "Why does your master eat with tax collectors and sinners?" Jesus, hearing this, replied: "It is not the healthy who need the doctor but the sick." He then added: "Go and learn the meaning of the words: 'What I want is mercy, not sacrifice.' And indeed I did not come to call the virtuous, but sinners" (Matthew 9:10-13; see also Mark 2:15-17 and Luke 5:29-32).

Another story about a tax collector illustrates the redemptive value of Jesus' meal ministry. As Jesus was going through the town, Zacchaeus, a senior tax collector and a wealthy man, came by. He was anxious to see what kind of a man Jesus was. Since he was short and could not see over the crowd, he climbed a sycamore tree so that he could catch a glimpse of Jesus as he passed that way. When Jesus came to the tree he looked up and addressed him, "Zacchaeus, come down. Hurry, because I must stay at your house today." Zacchaeus hurried down and welcomed Jesus joyfully and extended his hospitality. Again, some complained. "He has gone to stay at a sinner's house." Through the sharing of hospitality Zacchaeus was transformed. "Look, sir," he said to Jesus, "I am going to give half my property to the poor, and if I have cheated anybody I will pay him back four times the amount." Jesus replied, "Today salvation has come to this house, because this man too is a son of Abraham, for the Son of Man has come to seek out and save what was lost" (Luke 19:1-10).

The Woman with a Bad Name

Luke narrates another meal event that manifests the reconciling ministry of Jesus at table. This time it was a Pharisee who invited Jesus to a meal. When he arrived at the Pharisee's house and was seated at table a woman came in who had a bad name in town. Having heard that Jesus was dining with the Pharisee, she had brought with her an alabaster jar of ointment. She waited behind at his feet, weeping. Her tears fell on his feet, and she wiped them away with her hair. She then repeatedly kissed his feet and anointed them with the ointment.

The Pharisee who had invited him to dinner thought to himself that if Jesus were a prophet he would know what kind of woman this was. Jesus showed himself a prophet by reading the secret thoughts of the Pharisee. He proceeded to tell a parable about a creditor who pardoned two debtors. The one who was pardoned the greater amount loved him more. Jesus then commended the women for her expression of hospitality. "For this reason I tell you that her sins, her many sins, must have been forgiven her, or she would not have shown such great love." He then told the woman, "Your sins are forgiven. . . . Your faith has saved you; go in peace" (Luke 7:36-50).

The Last Supper

The night before he died Jesus shared a passover meal with his disciples. John situates this meal in the context of Jesus' enduring love: "He had always loved those who were his in the world, but now he showed how perfect his love was" (John 13:1). At the supper Jesus took some bread, broke it and gave it to them saying, "This is my body which will be given for you" (Luke 22:19). Then he took the cup, offered thanks, and gave it to his disciples saying, "Drink, all of you, from this, for this is my blood, the blood of the covenant which is to be poured out for many for the forgiveness of sins" (Matthew 26:28).

Jesus' farewell discourse at the last supper as recorded in John's gospel brings out some of the emotional dynamic that took place at the meal. It also points to the kind of personal transformation that Jesus wished to effect in his disciples. "Just as I have loved you, you also must love one another" (13:34). "Do not let your hearts be troubled. Trust in God still, and trust in me" (14:1). "I will ask the Father, and he will give you another Advocate to be with you forever . . . " (14:16). "Peace I bequeath to you, my own peace I give you, a peace the world cannot give, this is my gift to you" (14:27). "Ask and you will receive, and so your joy will be complete" (16:24).

Emmaus

On Easter Sunday two of the disciples were on their way to Emmaus talking about what had happened to their master. As they were talking Jesus came up and walked by their side, though they did not recognize who he was. He asked them what they were discussing. When they had answered, Jesus explained in light of the scriptures why the Christ had to suffer and so enter into his glory.

When they drew near the village they extended their hospitality and urged him to stay with them. He accepted their invitation. While they were at table, he took the bread and said the blessing; then he broke it and handed it to them. They recognized him in the breaking of the bread, but he had vanished from their sight. They realized that their hearts had been burning within them as he talked to them on the road. Instantly they returned to Jerusalem and proclaimed the good news to the apostles (Luke 24:13-35).

The Sea of Tiberias

Another post-resurrection appearance of Jesus that involved a meal situation took place on the shore of Tiberias. After the miraculous catch of fish, the disciples came to shore and saw there was some bread there, and a charcoal fire with fish cooking on it. Jesus invited them to come and have breakfast.

After the meal, Jesus evoked from Peter, who had denied him three times, a triple proclamation of love. He also gave to Peter the commission, "Feed my lambs. . . . Feed my sheep" (John 21:1-23).

Summary

Many times in the gospels Jesus is portrayed as being a dinner guest, as well as being involved in other meal situations. Jesus' presence at these meals always had a redeeming effect. Sinners were forgiven, tax collectors had a change of heart, disciples saw the Lord and were strengthened for their mission to proclaim the gospel.

The gospel accounts of these meal situations shed light on the redemptive meaning for us of Jesus' presence in the Eucharist. They also point to that eschatological moment at the end of time when the Lord will come like the master in the parable who "will put on an apron, sit them down at table and wait on them" (Luke 12:37).

REFLECTION/DISCUSSION QUESTIONS

1. Why was eating with sinners, outcasts, and disciples important for Jesus in his work of redeeming people?
2. To appreciate the opposition evoked by Jesus' table fellowship with sinners, put yourself in a similar situation. Think of three kinds of people with whom it would be societally unpopular to eat in one of today's more "fashionable" restaurants.
3. Explain what you see as the connection between sharing a meal and forgiveness. Illustrate by some concrete examples.
4. Read John's account of the last supper (chapter 13 through 17). In light of this account, describe what you think is the attitude of Christ toward us in the Eucharistic meal today.

Chapter 14
The Eucharist as Meal

The original setting for the Eucharistic breaking of bread in New Testament times brought out clearly the meal aspects. The followers of Christ gathered together in a home and shared a meal at table. During the meal the Eucharistic bread and cup were taken and shared.

The Mass as it came down through the Council of Trent in the sixteenth century had lost most of the visible aspects of a community meal. Since the Second Vatican Council an effort has been made to revise the Eucharistic liturgy in a way that makes the meal dimension more recognizable. In this chapter we examine three of the elements of a meal as they are found in the Eucharist: a gathered community, dialogue, and the sharing of food and drink. The chapter concludes with some practical implications for the celebration of the Eucharist.

A Gathered Community

A shared meal brings people together who are united by some bond. Several businessmen get together for lunch to talk over their latest venture. A group of professionals hold a farewell dinner for a colleague who is retiring after thirty-five years. A wife and husband have a candlelight dinner to celebrate their love. Obviously, these examples represent very different relational bonds. Each of these meals takes on a definite meaning precisely in light of the relationship involved. Each presupposes some degree of unity and commitment. The meal celebration, in turn, enhances the commitment and the relational bond.

The first basic reality about the Eucharist is that a community comes together to celebrate their common faith in Jesus Christ. There are several important elements that constitute the commonality that draws people together around the Eucharistic table: (1) their identity as Christians of a particular denomination; (2) their belief in Jesus Christ as Lord and Savior, and their faith in the redemptive value of his death and resurrection; (3) their desire to deepen their own commitment to Christ and to one another.

The Eucharist does not celebrate a perfect unity that has already been achieved. If we waited for perfect unity to take place, we would never be able to celebrate the Eucharist, for such unity can never be achieved this side of the grave. On the other hand, if the Eucharist is to be an honest celebration of the fact that we are the one body of Christ, there must be some degree of unity in regard to our faith and trust in Christ, our love for one another, and our commitment to promote the kingdom of God. Granted some basic degree of unity, eating the one bread and drinking the one cup in Eucharist will empower us to grow further in communion with Christ and with one another.

Dialogue

Another important component of a shared meal is conversation. Talking and listening to each other over food and drink is what gives a meal a distinctively human quality.

In the Eucharistic celebration there is dialogue. The first part of the Eucharist is the liturgy of the word. At the Sunday celebration there are three readings. The first reading by the lector or minister is usually taken from the Old Testament. The congregation responds "Thanks be to God." A further response to the reading is given through the recitation or singing of a psalm. A passage from one of the epistles serves as the second reading. The congregation again responds to this by expressing its thanks to God. The readings climax with the gospel. The congregation prepares for this reading by singing or reciting an acclamation. After the priest or deacon reads the gospel, the congregation responds to the good news by offering praise to Christ.

The homily that follows is meant to explain the scripture readings and to help the congregation apply them to their lives. When the Eucharist is celebrated for a small congregation (for example, at a retreat house) the homilist can sometimes provide the opportunity for the people to share some of their thoughts on the readings or to respond to the homily. This makes the homily more dialogical.

The final verbal response to the readings and the homily at Sunday liturgies takes the form of the profession of faith and the general intercessions. We proclaim our faith in God who communicates to us through the word Jesus Christ by the power of the Spirit. Since the message of God must lead to greater sensitivity and love for others, we then express our concern for people everywhere by praying for their needs in the general intercessions.

Sharing of Food and Drink

Preparing food and drink, offering them to each other, and eating and drinking together are indispensable elements of a shared meal. In the liturgy of Eucharist there is first the preparation of gifts. The bread and wine are provided by the free will offerings of community members. At the offertory the gifts of bread and wine are placed on the altar, and then offered to God and set aside for the Eucharistic celebration.

At the consecration the celebrant takes the bread and the wine and proclaims the words that are the sacramental sign of Christ's own gift of himself in the giving of the Eucharistic bread and cup. "Take this, all of you, and eat it: this is my body which will be given up for you." "Take this, all of you, and drink from it: this is the cup of my blood, the blood of the new and everlasting covenant. It will be shed for you and for all, so that sins may be forgiven. Do this in memory of me."

The important point about the Eucharistic meal is that Christ gives us more than mere physical bread and wine. Through this food and drink Christ gives us the gift of himself. He becomes the bread of our life and the cup of our blessing by sharing with us his truth, his love, his friendship. Through the sign of the physical nourishment and refreshment that bread and wine give, Christ nourishes our faith, trust and love, and satisfies the deeper hungers we have as human beings.

By personally participating in the Eucharistic meal and eating the bread and drinking the cup, we give our "yes," our "Amen" to the nurturing that Christ offers. We deepen our commitment to the one body of Christ. By sharing the one loaf and the one cup we signify our earnest intent to grow in unity with each other. In order to live faithfully to what is proclaimed in this shared meal, Christians must strive to treat and regard one another as sisters and brothers who eat at the same Eucharistic table, and who consequently are truly tablemates. To do otherwise is to make of the Eucharistic meal a lie, a sacrilege.

Practical Implications

There is a likely reaction that can be given to the kind of analysis just made regarding the Eucharist as a meal. "This looks wonderful on paper, but is certainly not what is experienced in the average parish on a Sunday morning." One cannot deny the degree of truth contained in this accusation. However, it is important to keep in mind that the meal elements are there, even if heavily obscured by the unwieldy crowds, the lack of real dialogue between priest and people, and the reduction of a loaf of bread to a thin and tasteless wafer. The appropriate response, then, to a theology of Eucharist as meal is not to throw one's hands up in despair, but to continue the work of shaping our Sunday Masses into true experiences of partaking of the Lord's supper. There follow three initial suggestions toward this effort.

1. A major problem with Sunday liturgies is that at least in the cities and suburbs hundreds of people who are virtually strangers to one another come together to fulfill their obligation. Since the parish is not experienced as a community of Christians committed to one another, neither is the Eucharist. Parishes need to be smaller communities where people have a chance to know each other better, to share some other facets of their lives with one another, and to be involved in a ministering way with those among them who are bereaved, sick or elderly, and those who have particular physical, emotional and spiritual needs. In this way the lived experience of community in our daily lives can be celebrated in a special way at the Sunday Eucharist. The liturgical celebration, in turn, can inspire and strengthen us for the sharing needed in our daily lives.

The practical difficulty with this ideal is that it calls for other changes. Ways would have to be found to make available more leaders of the Eucharist than present clerical structures and laws allow. There would be needed an expansion of the gradual movement over the past two decades of structuring parish communities on the basis of commonalities other than geographical location. Perhaps most difficult of all, there would have to be a willingness on the part of people to be more committed to each other and to minister on a regular basis to one another's needs.

2. Implementation of the first suggestion would make feasible the next suggestion. While the word ought to be proclaimed by the reader and explained by the homilist, the liturgy of the word needs to become a more shared experience.

The liturgy of the word is meant to be instructional and formational. People learn better when they are actively involved in the instruction and not merely passive listeners who give programmed responses. Homilies get low scores in most places because they seem so irrelevant to the lives of the people. Perhaps one way to remedy this situation would be for the homilist to set the stage with a two or three minute presentation based on the scripture readings. Then the homilist could allow seven to ten minutes for some members in the congregation to share their faith witness to the readings and to suggest further how these can be applied to daily life.

3. More needs to be done to bring out the meal aspects of the liturgy of Eucharist. What is called for here is an expansion of what has been done on a small scale in some places over the past two decades. The experience of participating in the Eucharist in a home ought to be available on an occasional basis to everyone. This would be possible if again the suggestion made in #1 were implemented. Daily Masses that attract fewer than fifty people or so ought to be celebrated in a suitable homey room on the parish premises rather than in a church that holds four hundred, seven hundred, or a thousand people. Finally, there should be provided a sufficiency of wine, and an adequate amount of bread that looks, smells and

tastes like what most people generally experience and associate as bread!

Summary

Three important aspects of a shared meal are the gathered community, dialogical conversation, and the sharing of food and drink. The Eucharist is a liturgical meal that contains all three of these elements. Despite this fact, large numbers of Catholics do not experience the Eucharist as meal in a very meaningful way. The question of how to bring the experience people have of the Mass in line with the theology of Eucharist needs to be addressed on a practical level.

REFLECTION/DISCUSSION QUESTIONS

1. Explain why the Eucharist is a liturgical meal.
2. Reflect on your own experience of the Eucharist. How does your experience compare with the explanation given in the first three sections of this chapter?
3. Explain your opinion of each of the three suggestions made in the final major section of this chapter. What do you think would be the advantages and disadvantages of each suggestion?

Chapter 15
The Eucharist as Memorial

At the last supper, after Jesus took the bread and the cup and offered them, he gave his disciples the command, "Do this as a memorial of me" (1 Corinthians 11:24-25). Sometimes we tend to think of a memorial as a commemoration of a purely past event. However, a memorial can also have a triple time dimension. It can commemorate a past event in a way that makes it somehow present now and thus enables it to affect our future action. In this chapter we reflect on the experience of remembering in our human lives. We then explore present and future dimensions of the Eucharist as a memorial.

Remembering

We commemorate a number of events that have particular meaning for us. On a personal level we celebrate birthdays, wedding anniversaries and silver and golden jubilees of graduation and of other significant happenings in our lives. On big holidays such as Thanksgiving and Christmas, we remember the events those days represent, and recall the happy times we had in the previous celebrations. On the national level we commemorate the discovery of America on Columbus Day, the country's independence on July 4, and the heroism of deceased veterans on Memorial Day.

In some of these celebrations of past events, the triple

time dimension of the commemoration is especially evident. Birthdays and wedding anniversaries can serve as two examples.

On birthdays we celebrate the past event of a person's birth. We recall the person's early years. We may even take out the baby pictures. In doing so we are also celebrating the present meaning that this person has for us today. The appreciation, love and respect we manifest on a person's birthday helps seal our relationship and assure further bonding.

Wedding anniversaries are another occasion in which the past, present, and future come together. What is celebrated is a past event, the day the couple officially and publicly exchanged their marriage vows. That event began a new relationship that the couple daily build together. In celebrating the anniversary of that day the couple recall this past event, perhaps look at the wedding pictures and share their remembrances of that day. They also celebrate the present reality of the relationship they now enjoy. Many couples use the occasion of an anniversary to renew their marriage commitment and to intensify their determination to continue to grow toward an even better marriage.

In our human experience, then, commemorations of past events play an important role in our life. They often help us to appreciate more the present, and aid us in facing the future with greater commitment and determination. This human experience enables us to understand better the uniqueness of the Eucharist as a memorial, and the past, present, and future dimensions of this commemoration.

Eucharist: Commemorating the Past

In the Eucharist we remember what Jesus did in the past. We commemorate an event that is now part of history. As

Paul made clear, every time we eat this bread and drink this cup we are proclaiming Jesus' death (1 Corinthians 11:26).

The death of Jesus, as a redemptive act, has two important aspects: the death itself and the free offering of that death. The mere act of dying is in itself neutral. All humans die, whether they accept that reality or rebel against it. What made Jesus' death redemptive is that he accepted his death as a consequence of the ministry he had embraced out of love for God and for all humans.

At the last supper Jesus offered in a ritual manner the death he would die the next day. He took the bread and the wine and offered it as a symbol of his offering his life for the forgiveness of sin, the reconciliation of humans with God and with one another. Earlier he had said:

> The Father loves me,
> because I lay down my life
> in order to take it up again.
> No one takes it from me;
> I lay it down of my own free will,
> and as it is in my power to lay it down,
> so it is in my power to take it up again;
> and this is the command I have been given by my Father.
> (John 10:17-18).

He had also said:

> Now the hour has come
> for the Son of Man to be glorified.
> I tell you, most solemnly,
> unless a wheat grain falls on the ground and dies,
> it remains only a single grain;
> but if it dies
> it yields a rich harvest.

Anyone who loves his life loses it;
anyone who hates his life in this world
will keep it for the eternal life. . . .

Now my soul is troubled.
What shall I say:
Father, save me from this hour?
But it was for this very reason that I have come to this hour.
Father, glorify your name! (John 12:23-25, 27-28).

At the last supper Jesus made clear through ritual that no one
was taking his life from him, but that he was offering it freely
out of love. He was demonstrating his willingness to die and
be buried in order to bring about new life.

The next day Jesus enacted the offering he had made at
the last supper. He accepted crucifixion and death. As he died
he proclaimed, "Father, into your hands I commit my spirit"
(Luke 23:46).

Every celebration of the Eucharist is a memorial of Jesus'
offering at the last supper and on the cross. Without the past
historical reality of that offering, the Eucharist would be a
meaningless ritual.

The Present Dimension

The Eucharist is a memorial that makes the past somehow
present. There was only one last supper and one death of Jesus. Having died once and for all, Jesus can never die again.
The author of the letter to the Hebrews contrasts the sacrifice
of Jesus with the Jewish priests who daily offered over and
over again the same sacrifices. Jesus "on the other hand has
offered one single sacrifice for sins, and then taken his place
forever at the right hand of God. . . . By virtue of that one sin-

gle offering, he has achieved the eternal perfection of all whom he is sanctifying" (Hebrews 10:12-14).

The Eucharist is not a repetition of that one sacrifice. It is a memorial of it. Because Jesus who died is risen, the Eucharist makes that past sacrifice present. In the Eucharist the crucified and risen Christ is now present with the same sacrificial love and redemptive purpose that possessed him at the last supper and on the cross. He continues to offer himself to God for us that we may become more deeply united with him and with one another.

At the Eucharist, then, we do not merely recall what Jesus did a long time ago. We come in contact with Christ who is truly present. We open ourselves to the present action of Christ who now offers himself for us and gives himself to us in a way that is in continuity with the love he showed at the last supper and on the cross. We unite ourselves with Christ in his offering. In a sense, we make his sacrifice our own. In union with his offering we offer ourselves.

Toward the Future

The Eucharist has an eschatological dimension, that is, it points toward future fulfillment. The crucified and risen Christ offers himself for us in the Eucharist, so that we might continue to grow toward greater faith and trust, and greater love and unity. Christ is present to us in the Eucharist so that we might become more aware of his presence in the totality of our lives. The manifestation of Christ's convenant with us in the breaking of the bread and the sharing of the cup is a pledge of his continued commitment to us. The communion with Christ and with one another that is experienced in the Eucharist points to the fulfillment of love that takes place at the end time.

When Christians celebrate the Eucharist they are also committing themselves to the future. In accepting the death and resurrection of Christ as redemptive, they profess their belief in the redemptive value of the dyings and risings that will constitute the rest of their own lives. Through participation in the Eucharistic sacrifice of Christ they commit themselves to share their lives with others. By being receptive to Christ in Eucharistic Communion, they intensify their yearning for Christ when he comes again in glory.

Summary

Remembrance is an essential element of our human conscious experience. In celebrating the Eucharist we recall what Christ did at the last supper and on the cross. This celebration is not a mere remembrance of a purely past event. Rather, in the Eucharist Christ is present offering himself with the same sacrificial love which moved him on that first Holy Thursday and Good Friday. The Eucharist also points to the future. It is a sign of Christ's eternal covenant with us. It also symbolizes our own pledge to be open to the redeeming and transforming love and friendship of Christ.

REFLECTION/DISCUSSION QUESTIONS

1. What is the significance of certain commemorations you celebrate in your family and social life? Illustrate by concrete examples.
2. Explain how in the Eucharist the past offering of Jesus is made present.
3. How ought the celebration of the Eucharist as a memorial affect the future direction of one's life?

Chapter 16
Real Presence

The last chapter stressed the fact that the Eucharist is not merely a commemoration of a past event. Rather, Christ now is truly present communicating himself to us in the Eucharistic celebration. In this chapter we explore the meaning of Christ's real presence in the Eucharist. Before doing this we first will clarify the difference between personal presence and local presence, and then examine some of the diverse ways in which Christ is present among us.

Personal Presence

To understand how the crucified and risen Christ is present to us today, a distinction has to be made between personal presence and local presence. Local presence means to be in place, as the Latin word *locus* (place) suggests. For something to be in place means that the extended material parts of an object are contiguous with the extended material parts of another object. A book is on this portion of the table, because part of the book is in contact with this particular section of the table. To remove the book from the table and place it on the bookshelf is to change its location.

People are locally present in the same way. One is situated in a particular area of the room; one is sitting in this chair rather than that chair, or is standing in this corner instead of in another corner. A person can only be locally present in one place at a time.

Human beings can also be personally present. We are personally present to each other when we are affecting the consciousness of one another. Personal presence is intensified according to the *degree* of communication that transpires between two people. The personal presence we have to strangers on a bus is minimal. Our personal presence to one another at a social reception is a little deeper. There is at least the exchange of pleasantries, even if it remains on a superficial level. Two close friends engaged in serious conversation experience a far greater degree of personal presence.

Another important point about personal presence is that one can be simultaneously present to a number of people. The lecturer, for example, is present to everyone in the hall. The degree of personal presence to each person in the audience varies according to the way the lecturer is affecting the consciousness of each.

The distinction between local and personal presence is important for understanding how Christ is present among us today. When Jesus died to this mortal mode of bodily existence and passed into risen life he was no longer bound by the dimensions of time and space appropriate to mortal bodies. The risen Christ, then, is not locally present. He is not bound to one place at a time.

Christ, however, is personally present to us. In faith he affects our consciousness and influences our lives. He is present at the same time to countless people everywhere. His presence to each person is unique according to the way in which people allow him to affect their minds and hearts and to influence their lives.

Christ's Presence Outside the Eucharist

One of the difficulties with devotion to the real presence of Christ in the Eucharist has been the fact that sometimes this has led to an obscuring of the reality of Christ's real presence in many other facets of our lives. The presence of Christ in the Eucharist cannot be isolated from his ongoing presence in our midst. Our experience of Christ's presence in the Eucharist ought, rather, to make us more aware of his presence in the totality of our lives. As suggested in the preceding section, Christ is personally present to us according to the diverse ways in which he is encountering us and affecting our lives.

In the Constitution on the Liturgy (#7) the bishops of the Second Vatican Council make an effort to situate the Eucharistic presence of Christ in the context of the wider presence of Christ in the community. Here we will note five of the ways in which Christ is present to us outside the Eucharist.

1. Christ is present with each one of us communicating his Spirit and transforming us with the grace of his friendship.

2. He is present in the gathered community. When we come together in his name, we are there by his power. He is, as he said he would be, in our midst.

3. Christ is present in the word of scripture. In the liturgy of the word it is Christ himself who speaks through the proclamation of the scriptures.

4. He is present in the sacraments. In baptism it is Christ who gives the Spirit. In the sacrament of reconciliation he is present forgiving and strengthening the penitent. In the anointing of the sick Christ exercises his healing ministry.

5. Christ is present in the ministering church. He it is who inspires us to serve. Through the ministry of humans to one another, Christ affects his transforming power.

The diverse ways in which Christ is truly present does not

take away from his presence in the Eucharist. Rather, understanding the richness of Christ's presence in human life can aid in appreciating the purpose of his presence in the Eucharist.

Eucharistic Presence

Let us say we are coming together to celebrate the Eucharist in a large room or hall where the Blessed Sacrament is not reserved. In light of what was said in the previous section, it is clear that Christ is already present, because we are gathered together in his name. He is present in the liturgy of the word. Christ is also present in the person of the presiding priest through whose ministry he now offers himself (Constitution on the Liturgy, #7).

At the consecration, through the proclamation of the priest, Christ offers himself in the bread and the wine. He who is already present among us now becomes present in a new way. This bread is his body given for us. This cup is the cup of his blood, his life poured out for us. We take and eat the bread and drink the cup, receiving the Lord into the innermost depths of our being. He is the bread of life who comes in the Eucharistic bread that we may have life in abundance. He is the fullness of God's blessings, and he comes to us in the cup of Eucharistic wine that we may drink deeply of his blessings and possess him as the source of our joy.

Summary

While on this earth mortal humans are present both locally and personally. When we speak of the presence of the risen Christ among humans today, what is meant, of course, is his personal presence. Christ is present to humans in all the many ways in which he continues to minister his saving grace. Within the context of the diverse ways in which Christ really encounters us, the uniqueness of his presence in the Eucharist can be understood.

REFLECTION/DISCUSSION QUESTIONS

1. Explain the difference between personal presence and local presence. Why is this distinction important for understanding the presence of Christ today?
2. Describe several of the ways in which Christ is really present to us. Does Christ's presence in these ways detract from his unique presence in the Eucharist? Explain.
3. If Christ is present to us in diverse ways, what is unique about his presence in the Eucharist?

Chapter 17
The Eucharist and Human Hunger

The most visibly recognizable hunger among humans is that for food. The baby cries emphatically to let us know of the need to be fed. The emaciated look of children in many parts of the third world speaks poignantly of their dire need for food. If we go too long without food, we become ill, we die.

While this hunger for food is most visibly linked with bodily survival, there are many deeper hungers that humans have as persons. Addressing these hungers is essential if people are to develop to the fullness of their personhood.

This chapter looks at some of these human hungers. It also probes the relationship of the Eucharist to these hungers.

Hunger for Acceptance and Love

One of the basic needs that humans have is to be appreciated and loved. We need to feel good about ourselves and to be esteemed by others. Everyone desires to be someone in one's own eyes and in the eyes of others.

Much of one's well-being depends on whether or not this need has been satisfied. Many psychological disorders are rooted in a bad self-image, which is often a consequence of not being accepted and loved by others. Anti-social behavior is frequently a manifestation of the same phenomenon. Without an inner security about one's own worth, it is almost impossible to take the risk to extend oneself to others.

The Eucharist ministers to this hunger for acceptance and love in at least two ways. First, in the Eucharist we commemorate Christ who experienced in an extraordinary way God's love, and who had so much inner security and belief in himself that he was able to give of himself even at the cost of being rejected and ultimately put to death as an undesirable. Christ's own self-acceptance inspires the Christian to believe in and to accept oneself. Second, in the Eucharist, the Christian experiences in an intimate way the acceptance and love of Christ who died and rose for us, and who calls us, as we are, into communion with himself. This experience of being accepted by Christ strengthens one's belief in oneself. It also leads the communicant to accept and love others as Christ does.

Hunger for Understanding

Another need that humans have is to be understood. We do not fully understand ourselves. Nor are we totally understood by our spouse or close friends. Children do not feel understood by their parents. Older people are misunderstood by the young. Misunderstandings block communication and intimacy. We often stand alone even in the midst of our friends. We long for greater understanding and intimate companionship.

In the Eucharist humans can find satisfaction for this hunger. One of the things that our faith presupposes when we participate in the Eucharist is that Christ understands our weaknesses and our strengths, our sinfulness and our goodness. The Eucharist celebrates the fact that Christ has truly identified with our humanity along with its fragility and vulnerability. He experienced what it meant to be human, even unto death. Through the sacramental sign of the Eucharist action, Christ makes clear that he is aware of who we are as humans, that he forgives us, and calls us to the fullness of our unique potential for good.

A community that honestly strives to live the Eucharist in its practical daily living ministers to the hunger that people have for understanding and oneness. To live the Eucharist implies understanding people as human persons with whom we share the basic human condition. This means putting aside prejudices that prevent understanding the basic human goodness in those who are different.

Hunger for a Purpose

"What is life all about, anyway?" "Is it worth it?" "Where does it all end?" These and similar questions have plagued the human mind down through the ages. People yearn for meaning in their lives. They need a purpose, a goal, some hope for the future. Without a purpose, life can just drift. There can be little motivation to work through the difficult times, and little desire to make the most of one's potential.

The Eucharist symbolizes the redemptive purpose of Christ. His death and resurrection, which the Eucharist commemorates, sealed the commitment he had to reconcile humans with God and with one another. The Eucharist sacramentalizes the ongoing presence of Christ who is intent on giving his Spirit to renew the minds and hearts of humankind.

This purposefulness of Christ inspires purpose in our own lives. First, in the Eucharist we affirm our commitment to participate in the redemptive mission of Christ. His goal of promoting God's kingdom becomes a central value in our own life. Second, the death and resurrection of Christ commemorated in the Eucharist gives meaning to the many dyings in the human experience. From loss and pain, offered in love, can emerge growth and new life. From that ultimate death that climaxes all human life emerges new bodily risen life. While there is no rational explanation for suffering and death, the celebration of Christ's death and resurrection in the Eucharist provides a meaningful context that frees the Christian to embrace life with its pain and its joy, its defeat and its victory.

Hunger for Justice and Peace

Despite the countless achievements of history, two failures have perennially plagued the human scene. Humans have been incapable of distributing equitably the rich resources of the world. A small percentage of the population controls and consumes the largest portion of the earth's goods. Secondly, the human family has been unable to live in peace. Wars have scarred the experience of almost every generation in history.

Yet humans have a yearning for both justice and peace. There is a deep instinct in the human that demands fair treatment. At an early age children manifest an uncanny sense of what is fair or unfair. No one wants to be left out. People feel they have a right to their share of the world's goods. Most of the conflicts within a family, in a neighborhood or among nations are the result of perceived injustices.

The human also has a longing to live in peace. Indeed, "heaven" or "hell" is experienced in our earthly lives on the basis of whether or not the environment in which we live is one of love, nurturing and amicable relationships, or one of hatred, bickering, and constant fighting. It is easily recognized that the former is life-giving, while the latter is personally destructive.

The Eucharist celebrates the fact that Christ died for all humans and that he intends for all people to achieve the fullness of life. The Eucharist also commemorates the reality that when confronted by the murderous attempts on his life, Jesus refused to retaliate. At the time of his arrest he warned one of his overzealous followers, "Put your sword back, for all who draw the sword will die by the sword" (Matthew 26:52). Jesus conquered enmity by loving, forgiving and praying for his enemies at the very hour of his death.

In order to be honest, the Eucharistic action of sharing the one bread and the one cup with each other must reflect the way Christians live. The concern at the Eucharist table that there be enough bread and wine to go around implies that in daily life Christians are concerned that the hungry be fed, that the thirsty have enough to drink and that the homeless have a place to sleep. Participation in the Eucharist challenges the Christian to work toward a solution to the problems of starvation in the world, pollution of the earth's resources, joblessness, and destitution.

The Eucharist is also an expression of unity. It presupposes a willingness to strive to live in greater unity and peace. The greeting of peace manifests our commitment to put aside what could alienate us and to work toward the building of peace in our relationships.

Summary

Christ is present in the Eucharist as the bread of life. In his earthly life he made clear that humans do not live by physical bread alone. That is true because there is far more to human living than physical survival. The human being is an intricate complexity of the spiritual, the psychological, the emotional, and the physical. Accordingly, a human has needs on all of these levels. We have spiritual and emotional hungers as well as physical. Human development demands that all of these hungers be satisfied.

In the Eucharist Christ comes to give us the bread of his own self. In his self-giftedness to us Christ nourishes us on every level of our being. Participation in the Eucharist implies that, in turn, the Christian will be self-gift to others. Sensitive to human needs, a truly Eucharistic people is committed to feeding all of the hungers that are part of the human condition.

REFLECTION/DISCUSSION QUESTIONS

1. How have you experienced the diverse hungers described in this chapter? How have these hungers been satisfied? How has your experience of Eucharist assuaged these hungers?
2. What are some of the other human hungers that are not explicitly dealt with in this chapter? How can the Eucharist help satisfy these hungers?
3. Explain why you agree or disagree with this statement: "A truly Eucharistic people is committed to feeding all of the hungers that are part of the human condition."

Chapter 18
The Eucharist and the
Other Sacraments

The Eucharist is the center of Christian life. That means that in a way it manifests in itself what all Christian life is about. On the other hand, the Eucharist relates back to and nurtures all the other aspects of authentic Christian living.

This centrality of the Eucharist is also true in regard to its place among the other sacraments. In this chapter we probe the relationship of the Eucharist to the remaining six sacraments.

Baptism and Confirmation

The Eucharist, as was indicated earlier, is the third of the three sacraments of initiation. In baptism one receives the Spirit and enters a new relationship with Christ. One also becomes a member of the Christian community that participates in an explicit way in the ongoing mission of Christ. Through the imposition of hands and the anointing in confirmation all of these aspects of baptism are confirmed in the individual. Participation in the Eucharist brings Christian initiation to completion, because it celebrates in a most visible and intimate way what it means to be a baptized and confirmed person. United with Christ by the power of the Spirit, new members take their place with the community, offering Christ's own sacrifice to God.

This action of the Eucharist is repeated many times in the Christian life. At each Eucharist the Christian reaffirms all the aspects of the commitment made in baptism and confirmation. In the Eucharist we proclaim our openness to Christ and our desire to enter into deeper communion with him. The Christ-life that is received in baptism is intensified in each Eucharist celebration. Our participation in the death and resurrection of Christ initiated in baptism is deepened by our commemoration of Christ's death and resurrection in the Eucharist. The Eucharist also reaffirms the baptismal reality of daughtership and sonship to God. In the Eucharist we join with Christ to proclaim God as his "Abba" and "our Father," and to offer with Christ his filial sacrifice to God.

Each celebration of the Eucharist also reaffirms our membership in the community which we entered through baptism. To be church is manifested most fully when Christians gather around the one table and partake of the one bread and cup. Each time we do this we own up to our identity as members of this church community. We commit ourselves to become more truly an authentic community of Christ's followers.

Finally, participation in the Eucharist reaffirms one's commitment to the mission of Christ to which every baptized and confirmed Christian is called. The word "Mass" which is often used to refer to the Eucharist is from the Latin word which means "sent." As Christ was sent by the Father to accomplish his redemptive mission on earth, so too every baptized person is sent to participate in this continuous work of redeeming humanity. Having commemorated at the Eucharist the climax of Christ's redemptive work in his death and resurrection, the Christian is sent forth, strengthened and inspired to proclaim and promote the kingdom (the reign) of God in today's world.

Reconciliation

There is a double way in which the Eucharist is related to reconciliation. First, unless some degree of reconciliation has been experienced when there has been a serious breach, the Eucharist could be dishonest. "So then, if you are bringing your offering to the altar and there remember that your brother has something against you, go and be reconciled with your brother first, and then come back and present your offering" (Matthew 5:23-24). As seen earlier, the Eucharist is a sign of unity with Christ and one another. Any serious disunion needs to be healed before a basic unity can be celebrated.

Even where there is no serious disruption in our relationships, perfect unity is never reached. Accordingly, certain rites of reconciliation are incorporated into the Eucharistic liturgy. At the beginning of the celebration the people are invited to recall silently their sins in a spirit of repentance. The congregation then publicly expresses a general confession of sin and a plea for God's mercy and forgiveness.

Another important moment of reconciliation in the Eucharist is the sign of peace, which is celebrated right before Communion. This begins with the prayer, "Lord Jesus Christ, you said to your apostles: I leave you peace, my peace I give you. Look not on our sins, but on the faith of your Church, and grant us the peace and unity of your kingdom where you live forever and ever." The priest presiding at the Eucharist then exchanges a greeting of peace with the people. The members of the congregation turn and offer each other a sign of peace. The people with whom we share this sign generally fall into three categories: those we love and who are an important part of our life, persons whom we know but from whom we are distanced, and people who are strangers to us. The sign of peace can deepen our intimate relationships, can help us accept better the people whom we tend to avoid, and introduces us to strangers whom we now have an opportunity to welcome. Because of this sign of peace we are better disposed to proclaim in the sharing of the one bread and cup that we are indeed the body of Christ.

This brings us to the second way in which the Eucharist is related to reconciliation. The very action of the Eucharist itself is a profound act of reconciliation. Sharing the Eucharistic bread and cup with one another brings us closer together in faith, trust and love. It is an action that implies forgiveness, acceptance, and a deepened bond between us. Participation in this action must inspire the effort to manifest this unity in practical ways after the Eucharist is completed.

Anointing of the Sick

Christ's redemptive action, which is celebrated in the Eucharist, addresses itself to all that ails human beings. The human person is a unique complexity of the spiritual, psychological and physical. What affects one aspect of our being affects the totality of our person. Accordingly, in strengthening our friendship with Christ and with one another the Eucharist benefits our total well-being.

As the revised rites make clear, the Eucharist, then, is an integral part of the ministry to the sick. The anointing sacramentalizes Christ's concern and healing power through the sign of oil. Communion to the sick makes Christ present in a unique way and is a sign of his compassion and love. The Eucharist, as a commemoration of Christ's death and resurrection, is also a sign of hope that can give redemptive meaning to one's sufferings. In pastoral practice the two sacraments come together. Ideally, the anointing of the sick is performed either in the context of the Eucharist, or is followed by giving communion to the sick person.

Orders

In the section on baptism it was recalled that through baptism all Christians share in the priesthood of Christ. The Eucharist sacramentalizes the priestly action of Christ who once and for all offered himself in sacrifice to God on behalf of all humankind. At the Eucharist the ordained and non-ordained members of the community, in their own way, manifest most visibly their share in the priesthood of Christ, by uniting themselves with him in his sacrifice. By virtue of orders the priest presides at the Eucharistic liturgy. The members of the congregation, on the other hand, join in the offering of the Eucharist by virtue of the priesthood which is theirs through baptism and confirmation.

Marriage

As the author of the letter to the Ephesians makes clear, the covenant relationship between wife and husband is a sign of Christ's love for his people, the church. In other words, Christ's covenant with his people is perceived in terms of a marital relationship.

The Eucharist celebrates this covenant between Christ and the church. "This is the cup of my blood, the blood of the new and everlasting covenant." The Eucharist commemorates Christ's offering of his life for us. In the Eucharist Christ gives the gift of his body-person to his people in friendship and love.

Since the Eucharist is a unique sacramental sign of Christ's covenant relationship with his spouse, the Church, the Eucharistic action is a model for the way wife and husband ought to relate to each other. On the other hand, the living experience of a couple's gift of their body-persons in marital love and in the totality of their lives together gives visible sign of Christ's Eucharistic love.

Summary

The Eucharist is the sacrament that the Christian participates in far more than all the other sacraments. Church-going Catholics will receive the Eucharist at least a few thousand times during their life-span. For such people the Eucharist is the liturgical mainstay of their growth in Christian discipleship. In the Eucharist the Christian reaffirms the Christ-life embraced in baptism and confirmation. The Eucharist is a profound source of reconciliation and healing, and a most visible expression of our participation, as ordained or non-ordained persons, in the priesthood of Christ. In a particular way a Christian married couple can experience in the covenant of the Eucharist a significant and enriching parallel to their own marriage covenant.

REFLECTION/DISCUSSION QUESTIONS

1. Why is the Eucharist the third sacrament that completes Christian initiation?
2. Recent surveys indicate a dramatic decline in Catholic participation in private confession, and at the same time a marked increase in full participation in the Eucharist. Does this mean that there is necessarily less sacramental experience of reconciliation today? Explain.
3. Show how the Eucharist and the sacrament of Christian marriage complement each other.

Chapter 19
Eucharistic Spirituality

In a sense, all of the chapters in this section point to a Eucharistic spirituality. Every aspect of the Eucharist treated thus far has practical implications for daily Christian living. Without unduly repeating the implications suggested earlier in this section, the present chapter explores how a spirituality inspired by the meaning of Eucharistic presence can be pursued.

Personal Presence

In an earlier chapter we saw that in the Eucharist Christ gives us the bread and wine as a sign of the gift of himself in friendship and love. What is of value for our personal transformation is not the bread and wine in themselves, but Christ's gift of self that is signified in the food and drink.

To believe in the Eucharist is to believe in the power of Christ's personal presence. Christ redeems us not merely by what he does or by the things he gives, but by being for us and with us.

To live Eucharistically means that we too believe in the transforming power of our own personal presence. It means believing that who we are is more fundamental and more important than what we do. The doing and giving of things have in themselves no power to enrich other people. That power comes from the gift of oneself in friendship and love. The things we do and give to others only have power to enrich the innermost depths of the being of another to the degree that they are signs of our being for and becoming involved with this person. If these actions become substitutes for the deeper gift of our personal presence, to that extent they lose their redemptive value.

Jesus touched the lives of people in a profound way because he shared himself with them. He violated the tradition of the time and spoke to the Samaritan woman at the well. He broke down the distance, entered into her world of belief and into her history of several marriages, and brought her into a new life of relationship. Whenever he healed, he refused to work magic. The touch that cleansed leprosy, gave sight to the blind, and stopped chronic hemorrhaging addressed itself to a faith relationship that already existed and was geared at deepening that relationship.

When he fed the hungry, he warned that physical bread, important though it be, was not enough. He became for us the bread of life. It is the bread of himself and his personal power that he gives us in the Communion bread.

The Eucharistic principle of personal presence needs to be at the heart of Christian action. It can transform every relationship and make it more fully redemptive. Several concrete relationships that constitute an important part of human life can serve as illustrations.

Marriage

In marriage the wife and husband exchange countless actions and things in the course of their lives together. Yet, in human terms, marriages yield dramatically different results.

Some marriages end in separation. In other marriages spouses maintain a protective distance from one another. Other couples achieve intimate personal communion. There is nothing magic about eating at the same table, sleeping in the same bed, and doing countless things for each other. All these experiences have the power to bond the couple together, to enrich them as people, and to bring them into a new life of intimacy only if these actions are signs of the lifelong gift of both spouses being for each other in sacrificial love. Relating Eucharistically is at the heart of a Christian spirituality of marriage.

Parenting

Parenthood is rooted in the physical reality of two people giving of their bodies to one another in sexual intercourse. Ideally, this also involves the gift of their total selves to each other in commitment and love, and the acceptance of their child as the fruit of this love. In other words, on a personal level, the deepest dimension of co-parenting is the couple being for each other, and, together, being for their child. This gift of personal presence transforms all of the physical actions we must perform for a child—from changing diapers and preparing meals to dispensing band-aids and providing transportation—from mere functions to expressions of sensitivity, love, and concern. When so transformed, all of these actions enrich and strengthen the personal bond between parents and child that will last forever.

This gift of personal presence also manifests itself in taking time to be with one's children. This often means changing our schedules in order to be available to our children when they have needs. It includes walking with them at their pace, listening to their stories, and sharing with them our ideas and feelings. It means playing games with them, helping them with their homework, and teaching them the skills necessary for performing basic chores and mastering certain crafts and athletic activities.

The sacrifice involved in being personally present to one's children yields rich fruit. Such personal presence has lasting effects on their growth and development. It contributes more than anything else to the building of mature and intimate relationships between parents and children. It is a most important foundation for the lasting influence that parents will have on their children, even decades after the parents are deceased.

Professional Relationships

The dimension of personal presence in Eucharistic spirituality also has application to our relationships on the job. The people who sit at the reception desk in a doctor's office, take orders at a fast food chain, or answer the telephone in a business firm perform similar kinds of functionary work. Yet they provide us with entirely disparate experiences, depending on how they present themselves to us. They can coldly stare at us or smile warmly with their eyes. They can gruffly ask us questions and give monotone answers, or they can go out of their way to express interest. They can dispatch us as another piece on the assembly line, or serve us with sensitivity and concern. While the function is performed, regardless of the manner, we are personally affected by the quality of their presence.

Turning to more professional forms of work, the same principle is manifest. The work of teaching is much more than imparting facts according to a pre-planned systematic program. True education takes place when the teacher is aware of the unique talents, needs and dispositions of this particular student at this point in time, and is sensitive to the teachable moments in the unique life journey of the student. The influential teacher is one who inspires through respect, concern, and acceptance of the student as an equal human person.

Recent studies have shown how inadequate health services are if they are directed merely toward remedying physical maladies. Sick people need to experience from those caring for them understanding, compassion and a practical sensitivity to their emotional, psychological and spiritual needs. The gift of personal presence to the ill is at least as essential as medicine and physical care.

Finally, the gift of personal presence is essential if welfare programs are to lead the disadvantaged to new vistas of opportunity rather than keep them entrapped in conditions of dependence and personal degradation. Food packages and money grants, helpful though they be, are not enough. The haves must be willing to walk with the have-nots and welcome them into their midst. Only by association with us and by integration into our environment of cultural, educational, and occupational opportunity will the underprivileged and disadvantaged be able to live a new life of independence and have access to the equal rights due to every human.

Summary

Christ in the Eucharist gives us not just bread and wine, but the gift of himself. To live Eucharistically means that one does not allow the giving of things and the being busy for others be cheap substitutes for the transforming gift of oneself to another. The material things and the actions become, instead, signs of the more sacrificial gift of self. The gift of being present to others radically transforms our marital, parental and professional relationships and enables us to be signs of Christ's Eucharistic presence.

REFLECTION/DISCUSSION QUESTIONS

1. Explain what it means to say that Christ transforms and enriches us by the gift of his personal presence.

2. Reflect on two or three relationships you have experienced in which the gift of personal presence was inadequate. How did this affect you? Also reflect on two or three relationships in which the gift of personal presence was most evident. What difference have these relationships made in your life?

3. Beyond the examples provided in this chapter, discuss some other kinds of relationships to which the ideas in this chapter would have application.

Part Four

RECONCILIATION

Regardless of how hard we try to build human relationships, we experience hurts and offenses. We need to forgive and to be forgiven.

In this section we wish to situate the sacrament of reconciliation in the context of the human experience of sinfulness and forgiveness. Chapter 20 reflects on the general conditions of alienation in the world and the need for reconciliation. The subsequent chapters consider the forgiveness of Christ in light of the gospels, the human experience of reconciliation in daily life, and the sacrament of reconciliation.

Chapter 20
Reconciliation in an
Alienated World

A basic element of our human experience is that we are
born into a world that is ripped apart by divisions, hostilities
and violence. In this chapter we probe the human condition
of alienation, first from a biblical perspective, and then in the
context of the contemporary world.

A Biblical Perspective

In Chapters 2, 3 and 4 in the book of Genesis, the Yahwist
author, writing in the tenth century B.C., depicts the original
plan of creation that God had for humans, and then contrasts
that with the condition that resulted from human sin. The first
scene is one of harmony. The second is a picture of deep-
seated alienation.

In the creation account in Chapter 2, the humans are situated in a garden in Eden. Scripture scholars point to two pertinent facts. First, the garden is a symbol of divine blessings.
Second, while Eden is an Akkadian word meaning "steppe,"
the author probably intended that his readers recall the similar
Hebrew word "eden" meaning "pleasure."

In the situation prior to sin the female and male are equal as persons. They are of the same bone and flesh. Marriage is the joining together of two equal beings who become one body.

Also in this original situation work is in itself good and consonant with the human condition. "Yahweh God took the man and settled him in the garden of Eden to cultivate and take care of it" (v. 15).

In Chapter 3 of the book of Genesis the Yahwist author narrates the origin of human sin. Humans refused to be subject as creatures to God as Creator. As a result they estranged themselves from friendship with God. Consequently, they were cut off from the garden. The relationship between wife and husband became mixed with alienation: the husband pointed the finger of accusation at his wife (v. 12); the man would lord it over his spouse (v. 16). This alienation between humans manifested itself even further in Cain's murder of Abel (4:8).

As a result of sin humans also became alienated from work and from the earth that they were commissioned to cultivate. The soil is accursed. With suffering humans will get their food from the earth which will also yield brambles and thistles (3:18). "With sweat on your brow shall you eat your bread, until you return to the soil, as you were taken from it" (3:19).

Alienation, however, was not to be the final condition of humans. The God of the Hebrew scriptures is a God of the covenant and a God of love. Even when humans are unfaithful, God is kind and faithful. God offers forgiveness and calls humans to be converted from alienation to reconciliation. Estrangement from God, from fellow humans, and from the earth would be lived out in the context of the universal call to redemption.

The Contemporary Condition

This is not the place for a sociological analysis of civilization today. We do wish, however, to reflect on four aspects of the alienation that pervades our societal experience, that threatens our collective well-being, and that cries out for reconciliation.

1. Widespread Violation of Human Rights

Nightly the pictures flash on the TV screen: babies dying from malnutrition on the streets of India, families living in dire poverty in Haiti, Catholics and Protestants killing each other in Northern Ireland, innocent people captured and imprisoned for political dissent in El Salvador.

Perhaps as equally disturbing are the violent acts against people that are not ordinarily recorded for television viewing. Daily, prisoners are beaten and homosexually raped by fellow prisoners, as guards stand by helplessly. Children are kidnaped and reduced to sexual enslavement by pimps and the entrepreneurs of the multi-billion dollar pornography and prostitution industry. Ailing senior citizens are neglected and maltreated in nursing homes. Children are physically and psychologically abused in violent households.

This widespread violation of human rights is not merely the result of individual actions. Much of the discrimination against the poor and the vulnerable is organized and built into systems and institutions. It is a collective evil that is more than the simple addition of individual acts of injustice. This abuse of human rights and the consequent alienation cannot be remedied merely by individual conversion. What is also required is a collective *metanoia,* a change of heart on the part of the human population as a whole.

2. *Sexual Discrimination*

The most general and deep-seated discrimination down through human history has as its victims not a minority, but a majority of the human population, women. In the biblical narrative, the first repercussion of alienation from God manifested itself in the male-female relationship. Throughout history, this alienation has perdured. The man has taken advantage of his brute physical strength and dominated the woman and subjected her to a role of subordination and second-class citizenship.

So profound is the male prejudice against women that it perverted the male perception of two very basic relationships to the female. First, the male could no longer own up to the basic human experience that males are born of females and are dependent on them for the reception and nurturing of life. Despite the clear evidence of experience, the male had to claim that originally the opposite was true: the male was created first, and the female was dependent on him for life.

This prejudice also clouded the male perception of marriage. Instead of marriage being accepted as the coming together of two equal persons, the male won the upper hand. For millennia, in many cultures, the wife was the property of her husband. He had rights over her, while she had none over him. While in most cultures today the husband is no longer perceived as owning his wife, he is still widely regarded as "head of the household."

The discrimination against women has also survived in other ways. Women generally receive less pay than men for comparable jobs. Higher administrative posts are far more accessible to men than to women. Many churches still limit the role women can have in ministry. In most states divorce laws are more favorable to men. The double standard in regard to sexual morality continues to exist. It was only a few years ago, for example, that a local city paper received a flurry of protests for publishing the names of johns who had been arrested in a particular area of town known for its prostitution. No such protest was heard regarding the publication of the names of the women involved.

Women and men were created as equal beings who complement each other. Discrimination on the basis of sex is totally inconsonant with this order and reaches into every aspect of human life. Alienation in this basic relationship is uniquely symptomatic of human sinfulness.

3. Nuclear Threat

Murder and war are the apex of hatred and hostility. They constitute the ultimate alienation. Instead of growing away from the senselessness of war, the "civilized" world has moved into a new age in which humans are capable of devastating more lives and resources within hours than all the murders and wars combined have accomplished in the history of civilization. Modern technology is increasingly forcing us into a radical decision. Either we abandon all war and search for a peaceful means of reconciling our differences, or we rush ever closer to the edge of nuclear holocaust.

4. Ecology

There are two ways in particular in which humans experience alienation from their environment. First, many are alienated from their jobs. They never see the completion of their work. They accomplish nothing on the job they can call their own. Standing on an assembly line they feel like cogs in a machine. Further, most workers have little or no say in policy-making and no share in ownership and profits. For many, the environment of their jobs has become dehumanizing.

A second form that alienation from the environment takes is the exploitation of the land. Instead of cultivating the earth and preserving it for future generations, the land is plundered for the present financial profit of a relatively few people. Resources are being used up without adequate thought of the needs of the masses and the consequences for the future. Because of greed the largest segment of the world's population is cut off from a fair share of the earth's goods.

Summary

The Yahwist author viewed the human alienation in the world of the tenth century B.C. He then proceeded to write a story of how alienation came to be. His theological point is that God created humans to live in communion. Alienation is not the work of God but of human obstinacy.

As we view the world of the twentieth century we recognize the same basic alienation of which the ancient author spoke. Sin against God and sin against humans are two sides of the same coin. Consequently, alienation from God is intrinsically associated with all of the diverse kinds of human alienation that have plagued our experience of life.

Humans, however, are not without hope. Despite the many depressing manifestations of human evil, Christ offers the power of reconciliation. It is to this reality we now turn.

REFLECTION/DISCUSSION QUESTIONS

1. Going beyond the examples cited in this chapter, reflect on two or three other forms of alienation that mar the human condition today.

2. Show by concrete examples how diverse forms of alienation are not only the result of individual actions, but also a collective responsibility.
3. Choose one of the alienations spoken of in this chapter and outline some specific ways in which people working together can bring about reconciliation.

Chapter 21
Reconciliation in Christ

At the same time that the Hebrew scriptures describe sin in the world, they also speak of the compassion and forgiveness of God. This forgiveness is brought out in a poignant way by the prophets. Isaiah has God saying: "Though your sins are like scarlet, they shall be as white as snow; though they are red as crimson, they shall be like wool" (1:18). Joel describes God as being "all tenderness and compassion, slow to anger, rich in graciousness" (2:13). Again, Isaiah has God speak: "But I will heal him and console him, I will comfort him to the full, both him and his afflicted fellows, bringing praise to their lips. Peace, peace to far and near. I will indeed heal him" (57:18-19).

Christian belief continues the theme of God's compassion and forgiveness, and sees the fullness of God's work of reconciliation manifested in Jesus. Christ becomes the living sign of God's embrace of sinful humanity. In this chapter we examine some of the dimensions of reconciliation in Christ.

Incarnation: Radical Reconciliation

The enfleshment of the word of God is the fullest way in which reconciliation with God is made possible to humans. As seen earlier in this book, in Jesus Christ humanity and divinity

148

are forever united on the level of existence. The word of God has become human. The humanity of Christ has become the new temple, the new dwelling place of God. God has touched all humanity through the humanness of Christ. All humanity can approach God through the humanity of Christ.

Jesus' Forgiveness

Some of the dimensions of Jesus' forgiveness, such as his reaching out to sinners and eating with them, have already been explored in earlier chapters. Here we can center on two narratives concerning Jesus' forgiveness of certain individuals during his public ministry.

The first is John's narrative of the adulterous woman. While Jesus was teaching in the temple, the scribes and Pharisees brought in a woman who had been caught committing adultery. In front of everyone they made a display of the woman and challenged Jesus to give his opinion on whether the Mosaic law that required such a woman to be stoned to death should apply. They did this to try to trap Jesus. He avoided the question by writing on the ground. Probably he was idly tracing figures to show his disinterest. When they persisted with their question, he looked up and said: "If there is one of you who has not sinned, let him be the first to throw a stone at her." As he bent down and wrote on the ground again, they each walked away. When Jesus was finally alone with the woman, he looked up and asked: "Has no one condemned you?" "No one, sir," she replied. Jesus then proclaimed "Neither do I condemn you; go away and don't sin anymore" (John 8:1-11).

In this event Jesus made evident his sensitivity toward the woman and his refusal to condemn her. Remaining behind as the only sinless one, he did what the sinful men would not do. He forgave her. In his forgiveness, Jesus offered the woman the opportunity for conversion and a new way of life.

Another narrative in the gospel about Jesus' forgiveness involves Peter. All of the evangelists record Peter's disowning of Jesus before the crucifixion. Despite Jesus' warning and Peter's protestations to the contrary, Peter three times denied his association with Jesus. The story, however, did not end there. Matthew and Mark record that when the cock crowed, Peter recalled Jesus' warning and burst into tears (Matthew 26:75; Mark 14:72). Luke adds a further striking detail, "At that instant, while he was still speaking, the cock crew, and the Lord turned and looked straight at Peter, and Peter remembered what the Lord had said to him, 'Before the cock crows today, you will have disowned me three times.' And he went outside and wept bitterly" (Luke 22:61-62).

In John's gospel the repentance of Peter is further manifested in the triple protestation of love. In his post-resurrection appearance on the shore of Tiberias, Jesus singled out Peter after the meal and asked him, "Simon, son of John, do you love me more than these others do?" Peter answered, "Yes, Lord, you know I love you." Jesus then said, "Feed my lambs." Jesus raised the question a second time: "Simon, son of John, do you love me?" Peter again replied, "Yes, Lord, you know I love you." Jesus then said, "Look after my sheep." When Jesus brought up the identical question a third time, Peter became upset. "Lord, you know everything; you know I love you." Jesus replied, "Feed my sheep." He then went on to explain the kind of death this love would involve:

> I tell you most solemnly, when you were young you put on your own belt and walked where you liked; but when you grow old you will stretch out your hands, and somebody else will put a belt round you and take you where you would rather not go (John 21:18).

In light of Jesus' forgiveness, Peter had a conversion of heart. He in turn would strengthen the community. Finally, Peter was to seal his own following of Christ by submitting to martyrdom.

These two episodes represent the kind of forgiveness that Jesus showed countless times in the gospel narratives. He freely offered forgiveness. The acceptance of his forgiveness involved repentance and conversion, and opened the way to a new beginning.

The Challenge To Forgive

Jesus' own compassion, as well as his belief in the forgiveness of God whom he called "Abba," inspired his insistence that his followers forgive each other. Jesus' concern about forgiveness is reflected in both his parables and in the directives he gave his disciples.

Three parables about God's mercy appear in succession in Chapter 15 of Luke's gospel. The first parable compares God's attitude toward sinners with that of a shepherd toward his lost sheep. When a man with a hundred sheep loses one of them, he leaves the ninety-nine in the wilderness and searches for the missing one until he finds it. When he finds it he joyfully takes it on his shoulders, and, returning home, he summons his neighbors and friends to rejoice with him. "In the same way, I tell you, there will be more rejoicing in heaven over one repentant sinner than over ninety-nine virtuous men who have no need of repentance" (Luke 15:7).

The second parable is about a woman with only ten small silver coins, and hence probably poor. When she loses one, she lights a lamp and sweeps out the house, searching until she finds it. After she has found it, she too calls in her friends and neighbors to rejoice with her. "In the same way, I tell you, there is rejoicing among the angels of God over one repentant sinner" (Luke 15:10).

The third and the longest parable is about the prodigal son and his self-righteous brother. The younger son left home and squandered his portion of the inheritance in loose living. Later, feeling the pinch of poverty he decided to return to his father's house, confess his sin, and ask to be accepted as a paid servant. While the son was still a long way off, his father saw him, and moved with pity he ran to him, clasped him in his arms and kissed him tenderly. The father's response to his son's confession was a command to his servants to bring out the best robe for his son, put a ring on his finger and sandals on his feet, and prepare for a feast, "because this son of mine was dead and has come back to life; he was lost and is found" (Luke 15:24).

The father's lavish forgiveness was in contrast to the older brother's attitude. In self-righteous indignation he refused to join in the celebration. So too is the magnitude of God's forgiveness in stark contrast with the human tendency toward self-righteous condemnation.

This insight into God's forgiveness manifested in the parables is at the root of Jesus' command that his followers forgive one another. In the prayer he taught, Jesus linked God's forgiveness and our forgiveness of one another: "And forgive us our debts, as we have forgiven those who are in debt to us" (Matthew 6:12). "And when you stand in prayer, forgive whatever you have against anybody, so that your Father in heaven may forgive your failings too" (Mark 11:25). What is the limit on how much to forgive? Jesus' answer is that there is no limit (Matthew 18:21-22).

Summary

Jesus practiced forgiveness in a striking and remarkable way. His forgiveness transformed sinners and brought them to conversion. Jesus also mandated forgiveness as an essential component of discipleship. He told parables that bring out in a dramatic way the extraordinary forgiveness of God. He then set before us God's forgiveness as a model for human forgiveness.

REFLECTION/DISCUSSION QUESTIONS

1. Is it difficult to believe in God's forgiveness? If so, what are some of the reasons for this?
2. What are some of the concrete ways in which our behavior manifests denial of God's forgiveness?
3. Why do you think forgiveness is such an essential part of Jesus' teaching and preaching?

Chapter 22
Reconciliation and Daily Life

It is helpful to situate the meaning of the sacrament of reconciliation within the context of the daily experience of reconciliation in our lives. In this chapter we recall the daily need for reconciliation in our relationships, the ways in which we celebrate forgiveness and "making up," and some of the dynamic elements that must be present for reconciliation to take place. We also reflect on two experiences related to forgiveness and reconciliation: guilt feelings and "trying to forget."

The Daily Experience of Reconciliation

In the movie "Love Story" the young woman tells her beloved that love is never having to say you're sorry. While one may be able to get away with that statement in a Hollywood production, it does not ring true in the daily struggle to build human relationships. To be human is to be fragile and vulnerable. We yearn for unity, and yet we make mistakes, we misunderstand, we are disappointed with one another, we hurt and sin against each other. In all of these moments, the security of our relationship is threatened. We must either make the free choice to allow the damage to stand and permit the relationship to be further eroded, or we can set about the work of healing. If we choose the latter approach, we can work through the hurt and build an even stronger relationship.

The first and foremost context in which most of us experience forgiveness and reconciliation is the family. There we spend much of our time in intimate living with people we love. We are exposed to each other in all the diverse moments that constitute the rhythm of our moods. It is in the context of our family that we can let down our guard and surrender some of our defense mechanisms.

In a happy family we experience love and the effort to please each other. We also experience fights, hurts, and the annoyance of getting on one another's nerves. Growth in family bondedness demands that we own up to those faults and mistakes that have hurt others. We need frequently to say we are sorry, whether the "fault" was unwittingly letting a door close on someone's face, or a deliberate harsh word, or forgetting someone's birthday. We also need to hear and say frequently the words "I forgive you." Reconciliation and growth in family intimacy also demand the sincere commitment to change what is wrong and to make up for the hurt.

This dynamic of reconciliation is experienced in each of the three basic relationships that constitute family life: the marital, parental, and sibling relationship. Each in its own way has its vulnerabilities and hence its own need for reconciliation.

In marriage two finite, imperfect and diverse human beings join their lives together in the hopes of growing in love and union. There are hopes, dreams and expectations. Most of these are realistic; some are unrealistic. Some will be realized, maybe even beyond our expectations. Others will not be achieved. Accordingly, even in the best of marriages, some disappointments, hurts and misunderstandings will inevitably occur. An essential part of any good marriage is the frequent sincere expression of apology and forgiveness. This is sometimes expressed explicitly and formally. At other times it is expressed implicitly in gesture and look, in a special kind act, in a shared meal, or in the sexual expression of love.

The parent-child relationship has its own unique dynamic. Parents can unwittingly offend their children by being overprotective or overpossessive. They can also offend by overreacting to accidental spills of milk or childhood silliness. Parents can hurt their children by expecting and demanding too much from them. Children, on the other hand, can take their parents for granted, forget to show appreciation, or react negatively when they don't get their way. Children can be trained to own up to faults and be sensitive to the consequences of their actions. It is, however, equally important for parents to admit their mistakes and to apologize to their children when they have overreacted and treated them unjustly.

Another kind of dynamic is at work in the sibling relationship. Jealousies, competition and fights are as much a part of the sibling relationship as the companionship, the love and the fun that sisters and brothers experience with each other. The art of family life is to encourage and foster the latter, and to guide children to work through the former. At an early age children can be made aware of when they are hurting or being unfair to one another. They can also be taught at a very early age to make up for hurts by gestures of affection and extra acts of kindness.

The human experience of ongoing expression of reconciliation in our daily family life prepares the way for at least occasional expressions of reconciliation in our family prayer together. In prayer family members can pray for the people they have hurt. They can, in prayer, ask for the forgiveness of God and of one another. As part of their prayer they can utilize some symbolic ritual of reconciliation like the sign of peace or an embrace. They can pray together for the guidance and inspiration of Christ's truth, compassion and love so that the family relationships may be increasingly filled with honesty, sensitivity, concern, and a practical love.

Experiencing Guilt Feelings

Tied up with our experience of wrongdoings and attempts at reconciliation are feelings of guilt. It is healthy to feel guilty when one has committed a fault. One *is* guilty and hence there is reason for the feeling. However, once a person has admitted the wrongdoing and has been forgiven, one ought to be willing to forgive oneself.

The kind of rational guilt feelings described above need to be distinguished from irrational guilt feelings. The latter can manifest themselves in two ways. An example of the first way is a person who was wrong, admitted guilt and has been forgiven by others, but still feels guilty and is plagued with a bad self-image. The second way of experiencing guilt feelings is when something happens that is not one's fault, but one blames oneself and feels guilty. The mother of a crib-death infant, the brother of a suicide victim, the spouse of an alcoholic may all blame themselves even though in reality they had nothing to do with the tragic situation about which they feel terribly guilty. These kinds of guilt feelings are irrational, that is, they are without reason.

It may take years for a person to work through irrational guilt feelings. If, however, we are able to distinguish between irrational and rational guilt feelings, we will not needlessly blame ourselves.

Another aspect of guilt feelings is in regard to our seeming inability to forgive. Take the example of a wife who tries to forgive her husband for his adultery. However, after the adultery has recurred repeatedly with no sign of conversion, she files for separation or divorce. Now she feels guilty that she did not forgive him. Or a grown man tries to forgive his drunken father for all the physical and psychological abuse he inflicted during childhood. However, every thought of his father is accompanied by feelings of anger. He feels guilty for his anger and his seeming lack of forgiveness.

In order to sort out the irrational from the rational guilt feelings in such situations, two points need to be recalled. First, forgiveness must be distinguished from reconciliation. God always offers his forgiveness. Reconciliation, however, only takes place when the sinner is truly repentant. In the first example in the above paragraph the wife forgives. However, reconciliation as a wife and husband cannot take place because of her husband's lack of true repentance and because of the irreparable damage his behavior has inflicted on the marriage. Second, it is necessary to distinguish between the willingness to forgive and feelings of anger. In the second example, the man has forgiven, even though he still feels anger. Forgiveness is an act of the will. Such forgiveness does not magically wipe out the feelings of anger. These may linger for a long time. Being willing to pray for one who has offended us is a sign we have chosen to love and forgive this person, despite our feelings.

Forgive and Remember

Perhaps one of the most harmful adages that have stuck with most of us from our youth is the saying "Forgive and forget." This saying goes against the human experience. Forgive we can, but how can we forget? Psychologists tell us that everything that has happened to us is recorded somewhere in our psyche even though we do not recall most of it. Also much therapy is directed at bringing out some of what is buried in our unconscious to the conscious level where we can deal with it.

Experience teaches that it is much healthier not to try to forget, but to remember with healed memory. Negatively, this means that we strive to remember past hurts without hatred and vindictiveness toward those who have offended us. On the positive side it involves remembering the hurt in the wider context of the good: for example, the virtues and good things that the other may also have done; the guidance, comfort and support of God experienced in the situation; the strength one acquired in working through the hurt.

Summary

Our human experience of daily living reveals the need we all have for apologizing for our mistakes and wrongdoings and for extending the hand of forgiveness. We also experience diverse kinds of guilt feelings. Some of these feelings have a rational basis and some do not. Also from our experience of human relationships we have learned that while with effort we can bring ourselves to forgive, it is impossible to forget. What can be done is to remember with healed memory.

Reflecting on our human experience of forgiveness is an important foundation for the sacrament of reconciliation. It is to this sacrament that we now turn our attention.

REFLECTION/DISCUSSION QUESTIONS

1. Recall a time when you experienced in a significant way expressions of sorrow and forgiveness in a human relationship. What were the elements present in the dynamics of that situation?

2. Reflect on an experience you have had of irrational guilt feelings. How did you cope with them?
3. Think of some situations in your life in which you have been wronged that you are not able to forget. Why do you think striving for healed memory rather than forgetfulness can be more beneficial?

Chapter 23
The Sacrament of Reconciliation

There is significance in the change that has taken place over the past two decades in the way we have come to refer to this sacrament. We no longer call it confession, but reconciliation. The term "confession" emphasized the telling of sins, usually understood in a legalistic way. In that context forgiveness was often seen in terms of having our sins taken away. The word reconciliation suggests much more. It involves conversion of heart that brings about renewed union and more intimate communion with God and with one another.

In this chapter we first examine how forgiveness of sin is brought about through the gift of the Spirit. We then explore further dimensions of this sacrament by reflecting on the revised rite.

Receiving the Spirit

Catholic tradition has associated the origin of the sacrament of reconciliation with the action of Jesus in his post-resurrection apparition to the disciples, as recorded by John. On Easter Sunday evening Jesus came and stood among the disciples in the room where they were staying. "Peace be with you," he said. He then breathed on them and said:

Receive the Holy Spirit.
For those whose sins you forgive,
they are forgiven;
for those whose sins you retain,
they are retained (John 20:22-23).

In breathing the Spirit on these disciples who had de-
serted him only a few days earlier, Jesus affected their reconciliation with himself. By the power of the Spirit they were
forgiven and brought to new conversion. By this breathing of
the Spirit Jesus also empowered them to forgive others.

Any reflection on the sacrament of reconciliation, then,
does well to situate this sacrament in the context of Christ's
resurrection and his bestowal of the Holy Spirit on us. It is the
risen Christ who encounters us in this sacrament. He forgives
us our sins not in some merely extrinsic or legalistic way that
would leave us inwardly untouched. Rather, our sins are forgiven by the power of Christ's Spirit who transforms us from
within. Our sins are taken away because the Holy Spirit, given
by the risen Christ, empowers us to die to our sinfulness and
to turn to God and one another in honesty and love.

A narrative in Luke's gospel can help illustrate the inner
transformation that is involved in the forgiveness of sins. One
day when Jesus was teaching in a house some men showed up
carrying a paralyzed man on a bed. When they could not get
through the door because of the crowd, they went up to the
flat roof and lowered him through an opening into the middle
of the crowd, in front of Jesus. Seeing their faith, Jesus said,
"My friend, your sins are forgiven you." Then to show to the
unbelieving scribes and Pharisees that he had the power to forgive sins, Jesus said to the paralyzed man, "I order you: get
up, and pick up your stretcher and go home." Immediately the
man did as he was told (Luke 5:17-26).

When confronted with this paralytic, Jesus first addressed the deeper need of healing. He freed the man from the crippling paralysis of sin. Then, as a sign that he had the power to forgive the man, Jesus cured him of his physical paralysis.

Jesus' coupling of these two healings, the forgiveness of sins and the cure of paralysis, sheds light on what happens when sins are forgiven in the sacrament of reconciliation. Christ touches us with his Spirit, freeing us from the alienation that prevents us from walking together in union and love. Our encounter with Christ in this sacrament enables us to follow him more fully as we pursue the journey of life.

Hence, the experience of the sacrament of reconciliation ought to be a joyful encounter with the risen Lord. It needs to be a celebration of the giving of the Spirit who frees us to live as sisters and brothers in Christ.

The bishops of the Second Vatican Council, in their Constitution on the Sacred Liturgy, gave a terse directive: "The rite and formulas for the sacrament of penance are to be revised so that they give more luminous expression to both the nature and effect of the sacrament" (#72). We now look at this revised rite as a further way of highlighting the meaning of the sacrament of reconciliation.

The Revised Rite

There are three rites for this sacrament: the rite of reconciliation of individual penitents, the rite of reconciliation of several penitents with individual confession and absolution, and the rite of reconciliation of several penitents with general confession and absolution. We will concentrate on the first of these, and later briefly comment on the other two.

One of the most striking changes from "confession" in pre-Vatican II times is the option the penitent now has of making use of a reconciliation room rather than a dark "confession box." This not only provides a cheery setting consonant with a joyful celebration, it also presents the opportunity of communicating with the celebrant face to face rather than in shadowed anonymity. This new setting also makes possible the full implementation of all of the options that the revised rite offers.

The revised rite of the sacrament of reconciliation has five main parts.

1. The Reception of the Penitent

The priest is instructed to welcome the penitent warmly and to greet the penitent with kindness (*Rite of Penance*, #41). After they make the sign of the cross, the priest invites the penitent to have trust in God. Any one of several formulas can be used. Two of the options are these: "May the Lord Jesus welcome you. He came to call sinners, not the just. Have confidence in him" (#68). "If you have sinned, do not lose heart. We have Jesus Christ to plead for us with the Father: he is the Holy One, the atonement for our sins and for the sins of the whole world." (#71).

2. Reading of the Word of God

This scripture reading can be chosen from a long list. The theme of each suggested reading deals either with forgiveness or conversion.

3. Confession of Sins and Acceptance of a Penance

Two of the instructions that the rite gives to priests at this point are especially worthy of note. The priest ought to offer suitable counsel to help the penitent begin a new life, "reminding him that through the sacrament of penance the Christian dies and rises with Christ and is thus renewed in the paschal mystery" (#44).

The other instruction regards the act of penance. The decree that accompanies the rite states that the act of penance should serve not only to make up for the past, but also to help the penitent begin a new life. The act of penance should correspond to the seriousness and nature of the sins. The decree goes on to state, "This act of penance may suitably take the form of prayer, self-denial, and especially service of one's neighbor and works of mercy. These will underline the fact that sin and its forgiveness have a social aspect" (#18).

These two instructions correct two inadequacies of the past. The first was the tendency of many (but not all) priests to cope with the long lines of penitents by "getting them in and getting them out as quickly as possible." The revised rite calls for a longer and more personal encounter between priest and penitent. Counseling has become more feasible now that the long lines have disappeared. It can also be more personal, since the sacrament may take place face to face. Many churches suggest making an appointment. This means that a greater length of time can be set aside to allow for more elaborate counseling. Counseling in the sacrament can also be more effective if one has a regular confessor.

The second inadequacy was the routine penances given. These were usually prayers. In one of the parishes of my youth one priest automatically gave "one Hail Mary," while another always gave the stations of the cross. It is far more beneficial when the act of penance is suited to one's particular sinfulness and need for conversion. If someone has hurt another, for example, a special act of kindness for that person is a more suitable act of penance than rattling off "five Our Fathers."

4. Prayer of the Penitent and Absolution

There are a number of suggested formulas whereby the penitent might express sorrow. One such formula is stated this way:

> Lord Jesus,
> you opened the eyes of the blind,
> healed the sick,
> forgave the sinful woman,
> and after Peter's denial confirmed him in your love.
> Listen to my prayer:
> forgive all my sins,
> renew your love in my heart,
> help me to live in perfect unity with my fellow Christians
> that I may proclaim your saving power to all the world (#89).

The priest then extends his hands over the head of the penitent. This gesture is very symbolic and recalls the many times that Jesus healed through touch. With his hands remaining extended the priest proclaims the words of absolution, making the sign of the cross at the invocation of the Trinity.

> God, the Father of mercies,
> through the death and resurrection of his Son
> has reconciled the world to himself
> and sent the Holy Spirit among us
> for the forgiveness of sins;
> through the ministry of the Church
> may God give you pardon and peace,
> and I absolve you from your sins
> in the name of the Father, and of the Son,
> and of the Holy Spirit (#46).

The penitent answers: "Amen."

The introduction to this rite presents an insightful commentary on these words of absolution.

> The form of absolution indicates that the reconciliation of the penitent comes from the mercy of the Father; it shows the connection between the reconciliation of the sinner and the paschal mystery of Christ; it stresses the role of the Holy Spirit in the forgiveness of sins; finally, it underlines the ecclesial aspect of the sacrament because reconciliation with God is asked for and given through the ministry of the Church (#19).

5. Proclamation of the Praise of God and Dismissal

After the absolution the priest says words similar to these: "Give thanks to the Lord, for he is good." The penitent responds, "His mercy endures for ever." The priest then dismisses the penitent, "The Lord has freed you from your sins. Go in peace" (#47).

The same general tone of this rite for reconciliation of individual penitents is found in the two rites for reconciliation of several penitents. The advantage of a communal celebration is that it brings out more clearly the ecclesial nature of the sacrament of reconciliation.

The communal celebrations include songs, a greater number of scripture readings, and a homily. The examination of conscience is facilitated by a litany of statements that suggest common areas of sinfulness. This is followed by a general confession of sins. In one form of communal reconciliation, individual confession and absolution is provided for (#55). In the other form, used according to certain prescriptions, general absolution is given (#62).

Summary

In the sacrament of reconciliation we make a confession and have our sins forgiven. The confession that is made, however, is more than a confession of sins. It involves a confession of faith and trust in a forgiving and loving God and in the crucified and risen Christ who is the source of redemptive grace. It is a confession of one's commitment to the ongoing process of conversion. Finally, it includes a confession of our desire to be transformed by the Spirit and of our intent to live in renewed relationship with God and with one another.

REFLECTION/DISCUSSION QUESTIONS

1. Explain the meaning of this statement: "Forgiveness of sins involves the giving of the Spirit who transforms us from within."
2. Compare the benefits of individual celebration of the sacrament of reconciliation and communal celebration.
3. How does the revised rite make this sacrament more of a joyful faith celebration rather than a legalistic obligation?
4. Reflect on your own experience of the sacrament of reconciliation. How does it compare to what is described in this chapter? What suggestions do you have for making your experience more meaningful in the future?

Part Five

ANOINTING OF THE SICK

Jesus came to redeem all evil. Hence, he not only forgave sin, he also healed the sick. He identified with our human frailty and our mortal plight by suffering and dying himself. Through his resurrection Jesus changed (redeemed, if you will) the very meaning of sickness and death.

The risen Christ continues to be in our midst addressing himself to the sick and the dying. We examine in this section this ongoing ministry of Christ. We first reflect on the human experience of illness and healing. We then consider Christ's healing presence in the sacrament of the anointing of the sick.

Chapter 24
Illness and Healing

Before explicitly treating the sacrament of the anointing of the sick, it is important to consider the wider human experience of illness and healing. This will enable us in the next chapter to situate more intelligibly the meaning of the sacrament of anointing.

In this chapter we first reflect on the human experience of illness and some of the dynamics at work in that situation. We then reflect on the general ministry of healing the sick.

The Human Experience

Almost everyone has been sick at one time or another, even if only with minor ills that lasted for only several hours or a few days. The throbbing headache, the upset stomach, or a brief bout with the flu has taught us how disabling even small ills can be. We find it hard to read, to pray, or even to talk very long with people.

Fewer of us have personally experienced prolonged critical illnesses that may or may not have brought us to the brink of death, such as a massive heart attack, cancer, or serious and extensive burns. Through our friendship with such victims of serious illness or our reading, we have entered vicariously into such experiences. Vicariously, too, we have entered into the experience of loved ones and friends whose terminal illnesses finally caused their death.

In light of these experiences we can identify some of the further ills that accompany physical sickness beyond the pain, the discomfort, and the interruption of bodily processes. Doing so will also suggest some of the deeper dimensions of healing that the sick require.

First, there is the tendency especially in serious illness to feel guilty. The ancient Israelite belief that sickness was a punishment for individual sins lingers on, despite the book of Job and despite Jesus' own insight in John 9. Confronted with the sight of a man born blind, the disciples asked, "Rabbi, who sinned, this man or his parents, for him to have been born blind?" Jesus answered, "Neither he nor his parents sinned" (John 9:2-3).

Nevertheless, people so often accuse themselves of their own illnesses and that of their loved ones. "Why did God let this happen to me?" "What did I do wrong?" Many find it difficult to accept the fact that vulnerability to injury, germs, and disease is an integral part of the human, mortal condition. While some illnesses and injuries can be direct consequences of foolish actions (such as racing across a busy thoroughfare without looking, or taking a long walk in sub-zero weather wearing a T-shirt), they are not arbitrary punishments sent by God for our sins.

Second, when one is ill, one has to cope with many feelings of irritation. The physical ill itself can put one on edge, causing crankiness and impatience. One can become overdemanding, can feel sorry for oneself and jealous of others who are well and able to do things one is not able to do. One who is ill can also become frustrated at being dependent on others.

Third, a sick person often experiences estrangement from others. Frequently, people who are well do not know how to handle the seriously ill person. Some are repelled by certain illnesses and disfigurements. Many do not know what to say or how to react to sick people. The tendency often is to stay away from an ill friend, or at least to avoid any serious, personal conversation. All of this can only deepen the feeling of aloneness that the sick often experience.

A fourth difficulty that the ill often experience is misunderstanding and impatience on the part of others. There is a tendency on the part of well people not to be sensitive to how it feels to be sick. A healthy person is frequently tempted to think that a sick friend is exaggerating the ills, or is a hypochondriac. They well might express impatience toward the ill because they are sick and because of the inconvenience they are causing.

Finally, the seriously ill person may experience a crisis of faith. God may seem very distant. "Where is God in all of this?" "Is God concerned?" "Is God being fair?"

This brief reflection on some of the ills that accompany physical sickness make clear that in healing another it is not enough to pass out pills and provide physical comfort, necessary though these may be. The whole person must be regarded and respected. What touches one dimension of our being affects every dimension. The physical, emotional, psychological and spiritual are intertwined. Healing, then, must be holistic, that is, it must be addressed to the whole person. It is this healing ministry that we now consider.

Healing the Sick

In the second century before the Christian era, the wisdom writer who authored the book of Ecclesiasticus expressed his own holistic view of healing. Here is some of what he had to say:

Healing itself comes from the Most High,
　　like a gift from a king. . . .

The Lord has brought medicines into existence from the
　　earth
　　and the sensible man will not despise them. . . .

He has also given men learning
　　so that they may glory in his mighty works.
He uses them to heal and to relieve pain,
　　the chemist makes up a mixture from them.
Thus there is no end to his activities,
　　and through him health extends across the world.
My son, when you are ill, do not be depressed,
　　but pray to the Lord and he will heal you.
Renounce your faults, keep your hands unsoiled,
　　and cleanse your heart from all sin.
Offer incense and a memorial of fine flour,
　　and make as rich an offering as you can afford.
Then let the doctor take over—the Lord created him too—
　　and do not let him leave you, for you need him.
Sometimes success is in their hands,
　　since they in turn will beseech the Lord
To grant them the grace to relieve
　　and to heal, that life may be saved (Ecclesiasticus 38:2, 4,
　　6-14).

The author urges the patient to pray rather than be depressed.
He speaks of the need of being cleansed from sin. He then at-
tributes healing to God who works through medicines and
through the medical profession.

Experience teaches us that when we are ill we need the
healing services of many people. While each is specialized in
one particular aspect of healing, it is necessary to be sensitive
to the total situation of the patient. Though the doctor and the
nurse must concentrate on the physical aspects of the sickness,

their kind words, encouragement and bedside manner affect the total well-being of the sick person. The minister who visits and prays with the person must be cognizant of the patient's physical condition and must adapt the ministering to that particular situation. Friends and close relatives play an important part in the healing process. Through their love and acceptance of the sick person they help the sick person's own self-image and self-acceptance. They give the patient a reason for wanting to get well by showing how important this person is to them.

Physical illness tends to drag down one's spirit and cause discontent and discouragement. On the other hand, melancholy and despair can cause or accentuate physical illness. In some instances, the psychological outlook of a person may be a deciding factor in whether or not recovery takes place. Two people may have a similar illness. One has great optimism and a strong will to live, and pulls through. The other is despondent and has nothing to live for. While it is necessary to avoid exaggerating the power of mind over matter, the relation between the two cannot be entirely ignored.

This interplay between body and mind underscores the necessity of a healing ministry that addresses both. Showing love and concern, praying with the sick, reading pertinent passages from scripture, helping the patient achieve peace of conscience and an awareness of God's presence and love obviously helps heal the spiritual dimension of one's being. It can also help one be happier and more content. It can encourage one to accept the realities of one's condition. Where there is hope for physical recovery, the patient can be strengthened to work toward that. Where there is no hope for physical recovery the person can be helped to face that finality in peace and with trust.

On the other hand, addressing the physical needs of a person also affects the spiritual and emotional dimension. If one feels physically better, is made comfortable, and is in an aesthetically appealing environment, it is easier to have faith and trust, to be aware of the presence of a loving God, and to feel good about oneself. Medical expertise, drugs, clean linens, cards and flowers, appealing food, and a warm bath and a good shave or hair-do address more than physical needs. They also help to heal the mind, heart and spirit.

Summary

This brief reflection on the human experience of illness brings out the interconnectedness of the body and the spirit. Physical illness affects our emotions and our relationships with God and one another. Emotional and spiritual difficulties affect our physical health. Healing ministry, then, has to address the needs we have on every level of our being. The services of the medical professional, the pastoral minister, the counselor, relatives and friends are all parts of the sacramental way in which Christ continues to manifest his love, concern and healing power to the sick today. The sacrament of the anointing of the sick must be understood in this wider context of healing ministry.

REFLECTION/DISCUSSION QUESTIONS

1. Reflect on a time in your life when you were quite ill. How did the physical, emotional, and spiritual conditions in your experience affect each other? What elements in the healing ministry did you find effective and which did you experience as inadequate?
2. Suggest some of the ways in which each of the following can more fully minister to the holistic needs of the patient: doctors, nurses, medical technicians and aides, social workers, pastoral ministers, counselors, relatives and friends.

3. Explain how all these healing ministries sacramentalize Christ's love, concern and healing ministry to the sick.
4. Why does a reflection on the human experience of sickness and healing help in understanding the role of the sacrament of anointing the sick?

Chapter 25
Anointing of the Sick

In examining this sacrament we center on three major points. First we reflect briefly on Jesus' healing ministry. We then recall some of the basic developments in the history of this sacrament. Finally, we look at the revised rite of anointing the sick.

Jesus' Healing Ministry

"At sunset all those who had friends suffering from diseases of one kind or another brought them to him, and laying his hands on each he cured them" (Luke 4:40). In this summary way the evangelist indicates that Jesus' healing ministry was more extensive than the particular cures described in the gospel narratives.

In light of the specific healings narrated in the gospel we know something of the kinds of illnesses Jesus cured and some of the ways in which he healed. He cleansed lepers, cured a crippled woman who was bent double, and made a withered hand whole. People as disparate as Simon's mother-in-law and a Roman centurion's servant experienced his healing power. Persons suffering from dropsy, hemorrhage, blindness and paralysis found immediate relief. He healed whenever there was need, even on the sabbath. He cured sometimes when he wasn't even physically present, though most of the time the sick either came to him or he went to them. Jesus sometimes cured by merely speaking the word, at other times with a healing touch, and once in a while through a more elaborate ritual, as in the case of the blind man in John 9.

Two important points regarding Jesus' ministry need to be kept in mind. First, the healing of Jesus took place within the context of his central ministry of proclaiming the reign of God, which as we saw earlier is a reign of truth, of compassionate love, and of justice. Jesus did not come to work magic. Nor did he make any attempt to cure all the sick people who were living at the time. He did not eradicate illness. Presumably all of the people whom Jesus cured eventually got ill again and died. What Jesus did do was to confront evil where he saw it, and to redeem the human situation by making present God's goodness and love.

A second important point is that a requirement for Jesus' healing ministry was faith. About Jesus' visit to Nazareth the evangelist makes the incisive comment, "He did not work many miracles there because of their lack of faith" (Matthew 13:58). On the other hand, to the woman suffering from a hemorrhage he said, "My daughter, your faith has restored you to health" (Matthew 9:22). Jesus' performance of marvelous cures was not a proof that would make faith unnecessary on the part of his followers. Faith is an essential condition for discipleship. Those with faith could be healed, and, indeed, in the process their own faith was strengthened.

The gospel insights regarding Jesus' healing guide us in understanding the ongoing healing ministry of Christ that is sacramentalized in the anointing of the sick. Christ's redemptive healing is directed toward the totality of our being. It is an integral part of his mission of proclaiming and furthering the reign of God in our lives. The healing of Christ takes place within the context of our own faith.

Historical Development

The classical New Testament text that gives testimony to an early practice of anointing the sick is found in the letter of James. "If one of you is ill, he should send for the elders of the church, and they must anoint him with oil in the name of the Lord and pray over him. The prayer of faith will save the sick man and the Lord will raise him up again; and if he has committed any sins, he will be forgiven" (James 5:14-16).

The history of how this anointing of the sick was understood can be generally divided into four periods. In the first eight hundred years of the Western Christian tradition, two of the main effects of the anointing of the sick were the restoring of physical health and the forgiveness of sins. From the ninth to the fifteenth century the emphasis shifted from an anointing of the sick to a sacrament for the dying. Hence the sacrament came to be called extreme unction. Its effects were perceived primarily in terms of the remission of sins and a preparation for the glory of heaven.

The Council of Trent influenced the way this sacrament was understood and approached during the post-reformation period up until the Vatican II era. Trent was influenced by the theology of the Middle Ages. However, it did not confine the sacrament merely to those who were dying. Also it speaks of the possibility of a physical healing when that is expedient for the health of the soul.

In the Constitution on the Sacred Liturgy (#73-75) the bishops of the Second Vatican Council state that extreme unction may more fittingly be called the "anointing of the sick." They also make clear that this sacrament is not only for those who are at the point of death. Finally, the bishops call for a revision of the rites of the anointing of the sick. These revisions were promulgated by Pope Paul VI in his apostolic constitution, *Sacram Unctionem Infirmorum*, November 30, 1972, and are reflected in the new revised rites which will be discussed in the next session.

The Revised Rites

These new rites are found in the document, Pastoral Care of the Sick: Rites of Anointing and Viaticum. A reflection on some of the major points contained in these revised rites bring into focus the main aspects of the present understanding of this sacrament.

There are four observations about the general approach the document takes toward this sacrament that are especially worthy of note. First, the document makes a real effort to situate this sacramental anointing within the context of the various ministries to the sick.

> If one member suffers in the body of Christ, which is the Church, all the members suffer with that member (1 Corinthians 12:26). For this reason, kindness shown toward the sick and works of charity and mutual help for the relief of every kind of human want are held in special honor. Every scientific effort to prolong life and every act of care for the sick, on the part of any person, may be considered a preparation for the Gospel and a sharing in Christ's healing ministry.
>
> It is thus especially fitting that all baptized Christians share in this ministry of mutual charity within the body of Christ by doing all that they can to help the sick return to health, by showing love for the sick, and by celebrating the sacraments with them. Like the other sacraments, these too have a community aspect, which should be brought out as much as possible when they are celebrated (#32-33).

Second, the priest is expected to attune himself to the condition of the sick person and to adapt the rite accordingly.

> When the priest prepares for the celebration of the sacraments, he should ask about the condition of the sick person. He should take this information into account, for example, in planning the rite, in choosing readings and prayers, and in deciding whether he will celebrate Mass when viaticum is to be given. As far as possible, he should arrange all this with the sick person and the family beforehand, when he explains the meaning of the sacraments (#37).

Third, whenever possible, this sacrament ought to be celebrated in the presence of members of the family and other representatives of the Christian community. The anointing can also be administered to a number of people in a church or chapel.

Finally, it is very clear in the revised rites that the sacrament of anointing is for the seriously ill, and that the celebration of the Eucharist as viaticum (that is, as "food for the passage through death to eternal life") is the sacrament of the dying (#175).

The sacrament of the anointing, when administered outside of Mass, is divided into these three main parts: the introductory rites, the liturgy of the word, and the liturgy of anointing.

Introductory Rites

The priest first greets the sick person and those present. He then sprinkles them with holy water. As he does so, he may use these words, "Let this water call to mind our baptism into Christ, who by his death and resurrection has redeemed us"

(#116). This is followed by a brief instruction referring to the classic text regarding the anointing of the sick in James' letter.

The last of the introductory rites is the penitential rite. This is similar to the one that takes place at the beginning of the celebration of the Eucharist.

Liturgy of the Word

The priest or someone else present proclaims a reading selected from a long list of appropriate Old Testament and New Testament texts. This reading may be followed by a brief period of silence and by a brief explanation of the reading applying it to the needs of the sick person and those in attendance.

Liturgy of Anointing

This central part of the rite begins with a litany of intercessions for the sick person. The priest then lays his hands on the head of the person to be anointed. This, of course, is reminiscent of one of the ways in which Jesus healed many people.

The priest then recites a prayer over the oil. If the oil is already blessed, the prayer is one of thanksgiving. Otherwise, the priest blesses the oil with these words:

> God of all consolation,
> you chose and sent your Son to heal the world.
> Graciously listen to our prayer of faith:
> send the power of your Holy Spirit, the Consoler,
> into this precious oil, this soothing ointment,
> this rich gift, this fruit of the earth.
>
> Bless this oil + and sanctify it for our use.

Make this oil a remedy for all who are anointed with it;
heal them in body, in soul, and in spirit,
and deliver them from every affliction (#123).

This prayer is followed by the rite of anointing. The priest first anoints the forehead, saying, "Through this holy anointing may the Lord in his love and mercy help you with the grace of the Holy Spirit." Then he anoints the hands, saying, "May the Lord who frees you from sin save you and raise you up" (#124). This rite replaces the older rite in which the priest anointed each of the senses praying for forgiveness of the sins performed through that particular sense.

The use of oil is not only biblical, but also highly symbolic. As the rite itself comments, "The Church's use of oil for healing is closely related to its remedial use in soothing and comforting the sick and in restoring the tired and the weak. Thus the sick person is strengthened to fight against the physically and spiritually debilitating effects of illness" (#107).

The revised rite also adds an important instruction for the priest: "If the anointing is to be an effective sacramental symbol, there should be a generous use of oil so that it will be seen and felt by the sick person as a sign of the Spirit's healing and strengthening presence. For the same reason, it is not desirable to wipe off the oil after the anointing" (#107).

At the conclusion of this rite the priest recites a prayer. The following is one among several options:

Father in heaven,
through this holy anointing
grant N. comfort in his/her suffering.

When he/she is afraid, give him/her courage,
when afflicted, give him/her patience,

when dejected, afford him/her hope,
and when alone, assure him/her of the support of your holy
    people (#125).

In place of this more general prayer, one can be selected that is specifically tailored to the concrete circumstances of age, surgery or terminal illness.

The liturgy of anointing is followed by the liturgy of Communion and a concluding rite in which the priest imparts a blessing on the sick person. One of the optional blessings summarizes well some of the effects of this sacrament.

> May the God of all consolation
> bless you in every way
> and grant you hope all the days of your life.
> R. Amen.

> May God restore you to health
> and grant you salvation.
> R. Amen.

> May God fill your heart with peace
> and lead you to eternal life.
> R. Amen.

> May almighty God bless you,
> the Father, and the Son, + and the Holy Spirit.
> R. Amen (#130).

Summary

Jesus' compassion for the sick was manifested in his healing ministry. As evidenced in the letter of James, the early Christian community continued this concern for the infirm.

The focus of this sacrament shifted in the Middle Ages from an anointing of the sick to a preparation for death. In the Vatican II era "extreme unction" once again became a sacrament of the sick. The revised rites bring out the purpose and meaning of this sacramental anointing.

REFLECTION/DISCUSSION QUESTIONS

1. Why does an understanding of Jesus' healing ministry as recorded in the gospels shed light on the meaning of the sacrament of anointing the sick?
2. What are some of the significant changes that have taken place in our understanding and approach to this sacrament in the Vatican II era?
3. Show how the revised rite of anointing manifests a holistic approach to healing.
4. If you were a patient in a hospital and a priest came in and suggested administering to you the anointing of the sick, what would be your immediate feelings and reactions? Explain.

Part Six

ORDERS

A twofold problem often obscures our understanding of ordained priesthood. First, there is the tendency to isolate ordained priesthood from the priesthood of all the baptized. Second, because of the way history developed, the Latin rite of the Catholic Church has inseparably linked ordained priesthood to a clerical celibate lifestyle. Hence, in the minds of many people the two have become confused.

In this section we will treat the sacrament of orders in a way that hopefully addresses both difficulties. We strive to overcome the undue separation between ordained priesthood and baptism by treating in Chapter 26 the priesthood of the baptized. In Chapter 27 we reflect on the ordination of bishops, priests and deacons, and the ministerial meaning this has for the Christian community. Finally, Chapter 28 takes up the two thorny questions that have received a great deal of publicity in the past two decades: the relationship between ordained priesthood and celibacy, and the relationship between ordained priesthood and gender.

Chapter 26
The Priesthood of the Baptized

In the section on baptism we saw that through that sacrament we become incorporated into the Christian community which is a priestly people. We referred to the classical text in 1 Peter and showed how the Second Vatican Council reflected on the relationship between ordained priests and the priestly community. Without unduly repeating what we have already said on this topic in Chapter 8, we wish in this present chapter to develop further the meaning of the priesthood of the faithful. In doing so we will reflect first on the priesthood of Jesus Christ. We will then probe how all of the baptized are called to share in this priestly ministry.

Priesthood of Christ

During his public ministry Jesus was not perceived as a priest. He was certainly not a Jewish priest, for he was not a descendant of Aaron. Jesus was perceived as a teacher, a prophet, a healer. The New Testament document that reflects on the priesthood of Christ is the epistle to the Hebrews. It will be helpful to recall some of the insights that this epistle gives regarding Christ's priesthood.

This epistle was written around the year 70 A.D. Some scholars argue for the late 60's, while others conclude that the epistle was written after the destruction of the temple in 70. While this epistle has often been ascribed to Paul, many scholars today would say that the author was someone other than Paul. The epistle was addressed to Christians most probably converted from Judaism. It has as its principal purpose to ward off apostasy from the Christian faith and to show that the old covenant has been superseded by the new covenant.

It is in this context that the author treats of the priesthood of Christ. Several significant points that the epistle makes about Christ's priesthood are worthy of note here.

1. Jesus was one of us. He felt our weaknesses and was "tempted in every way that we are, though he is without sin" (4:15).

2. Jesus is a compassionate high priest taken from among humankind and called by God to offer sacrifice and become the font of eternal salvation for all.

> Every priest has been taken out of mankind and is appointed to act for men in their relations with God, to offer gifts and sacrifices for sins; and so he can sympathize with those who are ignorant or uncertain because he too lives in the limitations of weakness. That is why he has to make sin offerings for himself as well as for the people. No one takes this honor on himself, but each one is called by God, as Aaron was. Nor did Christ give himself the glory of becoming high priest, but he had it from the one who said to him: "You are my son; today I have become your father," and in another text: "You are a priest of the order of Melchizedek, and for ever." During his life on earth, he offered up prayer and entreaty, aloud and in silent tears, to the one who had the power to save him out of death, and he submitted so humbly that his prayer was heard. Although he was Son, he learned to obey through suffering; but having been made perfect, he became for all who obey him the source of eternal salvation and was acclaimed by

God with the title of high priest of the order of Melchizedek (Hebrews 5:1-10).

3. Christ's priesthood, which is of "the same order as Melchizedek," replaces the levitical priesthood of the old law which was of the order of Aaron. Christ is a priest "not by virtue of a law about physical descent, but by the power of an indestructible life" (7:16). "The earlier commandment is thus abolished, because it was neither effective nor useful, since the law could not make anyone perfect; but now this commandment is replaced by something better—the hope that brings us nearer to God" (7:18-19).

4. Christ's priesthood is unchanging and forever. "The others, indeed, were made priests without any oath; but he with an oath sworn by the one who declared to him: 'The Lord has sworn an oath which he will never retract: you are a priest, and for ever' " (7:21). In the past there used to be a great number of levitical priests, because death put an end to each of them. In contrast, Christ, because he remains forever, can never lose his priesthood. His power to save "is utterly certain, since he is living for ever to intercede for all who come to God through him" (7:25). Christ "has offered one single sacrifice for sins, and then taken his place for ever, at the right hand of God" (10:12).

The priest is a mediator between God and humans. In the old covenant the appointed priest entered the holy of holies in place of the people and interceded for them. Jesus Christ became priest in a new sense. Through his incarnation, death and resurrection the divine and human have come together in a new way. Being the enfleshment of God's word, Jesus responded in his life and ministry with total love even unto death on a cross. Through his death, accepted and offered in love, he passed into bodily risen life where he is totally with God and with us. He is the one through whom we now have access to God and through whom we will ultimately enter the "holy of holies" in our own death and resurrection.

The Priesthood of the Baptized

Christian priesthood, then, is not something over and above the priesthood of Christ or something added to it. Christ continues as the one priest. The community of the baptized, incorporated into the body of Christ, participate, by virtue of their baptism, in his one priesthood. Three aspects of this participation in Christ's mediating role can be specified here: giving witness, reconciliation, and the offering of worship. While these, of course, overlap, each can be considered individually.

Giving Witness

Earlier in the book we spoke about the Christian community being a sacrament of Christ to the world. By their explicit profession of faith in Christ, proclaimed both in the word and by the way they live, Christians give witness to the world of Christ's presence and love. Hence, what was said about the community of Christian believers being the sacrament of Christ speaks also of their priestly mission. By being consciously united to Christ in faithful commitment and love, and by manifesting this commitment, baptized Christians are, if you will, a mediating instrument through whom Christ reveals himself to others and through whom Christ draws others to himself.

Reconciliation

This witness is one way that Christians participate in Christ's work of reconciling all humanity with himself, with the God he calls "Abba," and with one another. Linked with this witness is the call that the followers of Christ have as peacemakers. Christians participate in the priestly work of Christ by actively working at the art of creating peace. Peace is never merely a given that can be preserved. It needs always to be created by confronting evil and injustice, by compassion and forgiveness, by loving the enemy, and by reaching out and touching the "untouchables." When Christians respond to this baptismal call, they are actively participating in Christ's priestly work of reconciliation.

Worship

Another essential way in which baptized Christians participate in the priesthood of Christ is through worship. This is especially true when the Christian community gathers together for the celebration of the Eucharist and the other sacraments. Worship also takes place when two or three gather in prayer, or when one alone worships in the privacy of one's own heart. This Christian worship is a prayer of faith, trust and love that acknowledges God as the source of all life and as the Abba of Jesus Christ. It is also prayer of thanksgiving and of intercession. It is prayer that asks for forgiveness and offers the dedication of our own lives in sacrificial love.

Summary

In Christian belief Christ is the one priest. He has revealed God to us and leads us to God. All of the members of the Christian community, by virtue of their baptism, participate in the priesthood of Christ. All are called to give witness, to work for the reconciliation of humanity, and to worship through Christ, with Christ, and in him.

The priesthood of the faithful, rather than obscuring ordained ministry, places it in proper perspective. The next chapter examines the ministry to which certain members of the baptized are ordained.

REFLECTION/DISCUSSION QUESTIONS

1. Explain what it means to say that all Christian priesthood is rooted in Christ, the one priest.
2. In what way do you think that the priesthood of all the baptized is presently recognized by church officials? In what ways is it not recognized?
3. Suggest some practical ways in which you think that the priesthood of the non-ordained and that of the ordained can be exercised in a more complementary way.

Chapter 27
Holy Orders

As a result of the Second Vatican Council, major changes were made regarding the structure of holy orders that had been familiar to Catholics of the Latin rite for a number of centuries. Prior to that year one entered the clerical state through a ceremony called tonsure in which some of the hair was taken from the candidate's head. There were seven orders. The offices of porter, reader, exorcist, and acolyte were called minor orders. Subdiaconate, diaconate and presbyterate were the major orders. Generally the minor orders were reserved to those who received them on the way to the priesthood. Similarly, only those who were going to be priests would be ordained to the subdiaconate and the diaconate.

On August 15, 1972 Pope Paul VI issued an apostolic letter *Ministeria Quaedam* in which he reformed the discipline of ministries in several ways that are particularly pertinent to our purposes here. First, tonsure is no longer conferred. Entrance into the clerical state is joined to the diaconate. Second, the four minor orders are replaced by two ministries, that of reader and acolyte. These are no longer called minor orders, and the conferring of them is no longer called "ordination" but "institution." Third, the major order of subdiaconate no longer exists. The functions previously committed to the subdeacon are now entrusted to the reader and acolyte. Finally, the ministries of reader and lector are no longer reserved to candidates for the sacrament of orders.

Presently, therefore, there are two orders, diaconate and presbyterate. The permanent diaconate has been restored. Accordingly, it is no longer reserved for candidates to the priesthood. The order of presbyterate includes bishops and priests. In this chapter we will reflect on the ordination of deacons, priests and bishops.

Deacons

The ministry of service to which deacons are ordained is described by the Second Vatican Council in the Constitution of the Church. They "serve the people of God in the ministry of the liturgy of the word, and of charity. It is the duty of the deacon . . . to administer baptism solemnly, to be custodian and dispenser of the Eucharist, to assist and bless marriages in the name of the Church, to bring viaticum to the dying, to read the sacred scripture to the faithful, to instruct and exhort the people, to preside at the worship and prayer of the faithful, to administer sacramentals, and to officiate at funeral and burial services" (#29).

The deacon is ordained through the laying on of hands by the bishop, followed by these words in the prayer of consecration: "Lord, send forth upon him the Holy Spirit, that he may be strengthened by the gift of your sevenfold grace to carry out faithfully the work of the ministry" (Ordination of a Deacon, #21). After having conferred the sacrament, the bishop continues to pray that the deacon "excel in every virtue, in love that is sincere, in concern for the sick and the poor, in unassuming authority, and in holiness of life" (#21).

Priests

In the Decree on the Ministry and Life of Priests the Second Vatican Council described the three ministerial functions of priests. As ministers of God's word, they preach the gospel. They preside at the celebration of the Eucharist and are ministers of other sacraments, especially baptism, reconciliation and the anointing of the sick. They exercise a role of leadership in the faith community, or, in the words of the Council document, "they gather God's family together as a brotherhood of living unity" (#6).

These three priestly functions are also emphasized in the bishop's homily as suggested in the revised rite, Ordination of a Priest (#14). Addressing the candidates for priesthood the bishop says: "You must apply your energies to the duty of teaching in the name of Christ, the chief Teacher. Share with all mankind the word of God you have received with joy. Meditate on the law of God, believe what you read, teach what you believe, and put into practice what you teach." The homily goes on to say that what the priest teaches ought to be true nourishment for the people, and needs to be taught not only by word but also by the example of the priest's actions and his life.

The bishop then speaks of the priestly mission "of sanctifying in the power of Christ": "When you baptize, you will bring men and women into the people of God. In the sacrament of penance, you will forgive sins in the name of Christ and the Church. With holy oil you will relieve and console the sick. You will celebrate the liturgy and offer thanks and praise to God throughout the day, praying not only for the people of God but for the whole world."

The bishop concludes his homily by describing the third priestly function. The priest, sharing in the work of Christ the Shepherd, and united with his bishop, must seek "to bring the faithful together into a unified family and to lead them effectively, through Christ and in the Holy Spirit, to God the Father." The priest is challenged to remember the example of the Good Shepherd who came not to be served but to serve, and who sought out and rescued those who were lost.

Later in the ceremony the priest is ordained through the laying on of hands followed by these words of the prayer of consecration: "Almighty Father, grant to this servant of yours the dignity of the priesthood. Renew within him the spirit of holiness. As a co-worker with the order of bishops may he be faithful to the ministry that he receives from you, Lord God, and be to others a model of right conduct" (#22). There follows the investiture with the stole and chasuble, the anointing of hands, the presentation of the bread and wine, and the kiss of peace. The newly ordained priest then concelebrates his first Mass with the bishop.

Bishops

In the Constitution on the Church the Second Vatican Council teaches that "by episcopal consecration is conferred the fullness of the sacrament of orders, that fullness which in the Church's liturgical practice and in the language of the holy Fathers of the Church is undoubtedly called the high priesthood, the apex of the sacred ministry" (#21). Episcopal consecration, the Council continues, confers the three offices of sanctifying, of teaching, and of governing. The document further points out that these three offices, "of their very nature, can be excercised only in hierarchical communion with the head and the members of the college (of bishops). For from tradition, which is expressed especially in liturgical rites and in the practice of the Church both of the East and of the West, it is clear that, by means of the imposition of hands and the words of (episcopal) consecration, the grace of the Holy Spirit is so conferred, and the sacred character so impressed, that bishops in an eminent and visible way undertake Christ's own role as Teacher, Shepherd, and High Priest, and that they act in his person" (#21).

In the revised rite of the Ordination of a Bishop, the suggested homily in section 18 that is addressed to the bishop-elect sheds further light on the episcopal ministry. "The title of bishop is one not of honor, but of function, and therefore a bishop should strive to serve rather than to rule. . . . Proclaim the message whether it is welcome or unwelcome; correct error with unfailing patience and teaching. Pray and offer sacrifice for the people committed to your care. . . ." The homily goes on to urge the bishop to be "a faithful overseer and guardian," and to love all those in his care including "the poor and infirm, the strangers and the homeless." The homily concludes in these words: "Attend to the whole flock in which the Holy Spirit appoints you as overseer of the Church of God—in the name of the Father, whose image you personify in the Church—and in the name of his Son, Jesus Christ, whose role of Teacher, Priest and Shepherd you undertake—and in the name of the Holy Spirit, who gives life to the Church of Christ and supports our weakness with his strength."

The bishop-elect is ordained by the laying on of hands and these words in the prayer of consecration: "So now pour out upon this chosen one that power which is from you, the governing Spirit whom you gave to your beloved Son, Jesus Christ, the Spirit given by him to the holy apostles, who founded the Church in every place to be your temple for the unceasing glory and praise of your name" (#26).

The new bishop is then anointed on the head and presented with the book of the gospels. There follows the investiture with ring, miter and pastoral staff. The ring is given with these words: "Take this ring, the seal of your fidelity. With faith and love protect the bride of God, his holy Church" (#30). The miter is placed on the new bishop's head in silence. The giving of the staff is accompanied by these words: "Take this staff as a sign of your pastoral office: keep watch over the whole flock in which the Holy Spirit has appointed you to shepherd the Church of God" (#32). The new bishop is then led to the bishop's chair. This is followed by the greeting of peace and the concelebration of the Eucharist.

Summary

The seven orders of a previous era have been simplified in the post-Vatican II era to the two orders of diaconate and presbyterate. The rites of ordination, revised in light of the Second Vatican Council, clarify the specific ministerial functions of deacons, priests and bishops. These ordained ministers perform in a unique way their role of service so that the entire community of the baptized may be led and inspired to participate in the ongoing prophetic, priestly and kingly mission of Christ.

REFLECTION/DISCUSSION QUESTIONS

1. Explain some of the major changes that have taken place regarding the sacrament of orders in the post-Vatican II era.
2. How are the ministerial functions of deacons, priests and bishops related to each other?
3. In what specific ways do the mission of the baptized non-ordained and that of the ordained complement each other?

Chapter 28
Who Can Be Ordained?

There are two long-standing prohibitions regarding apt candidates for orders. One is the law in the Latin rite prohibiting married men from being ordained priests or bishops. The second is the even older prohibition against the admission of women to any orders. Since Vatican II both prohibitions have become increasingly controverted within the Catholic Church. For a while it was hoped that if both controversies were stonewalled rather than seriously discussed they would go away. They have not.

There is often an interrelation between the way one understands the sacrament of orders and the opinion one has regarding these two prohibitions. Accordingly, this section of the book would not be complete without presenting some theological analysis of both current issues.

Married Priests?

The present law in the Latin rite that forbids married persons from being ordained as priests or bishops goes back to the twelfth century. There is total agreement that the origins of this prohibition is later ecclesiastical law, and not the prescription of Christ. It is also evident that in new Testament times married persons were chosen to be elders (presbyters) and deacons (see 1 Timothy 3:1-13; Titus 1:5-9). The Catholic Church in the East has continued the tradition of a married clergy.

The following are some of the major reasons most often heard for maintaining the law in the Latin rite that makes celibacy a requirement for ordination as a priest and bishop.

1. Jesus was celibate. It is fitting that those who participate in a special way in the priesthood of Christ as ordained priests and bishops imitate Jesus in this matter.

2. The priest should be dedicated to God with "undivided heart," and be concerned about "the things of God" and not the things of this earth.

3. The priest, as a celibate, is to give a sign of the kingdom of heaven, where there will be "no giving or taking in marriage."

4. The priest ought to be available for service to the people. In marriage one must be concerned about one's spouse and children. As a celibate the priest is freed from those obligations and is thus able to dedicate himself more fully to serving his parishioners.

5. The priest by his celibacy can be a witness to married people and to singles of the chastity they should be living.

These reasons, convincing as they may have been to many, especially in the past, have not gone unchallenged. The following objections can be raised regarding each of the reasons presented above.

1. Yes, Jesus was celibate. At the same time he did not require celibacy for his apostles and disciples.

2. The ideal of being dedicated to God with "undivided heart" applies not only to priests but to all the baptized. Jesus presented as the ideal for all his followers the challenge: "You must therefore be perfect just as your heavenly Father is perfect" (Matthew 5:48). The greatest of all the commandments is incumbent on all: "You must love the Lord your God with all

your heart, with all your soul, and with all your mind" (Matthew 22:37). Love of other humans is not perceived as being in conflict with love of God but rather is demanded by it. Hence, Jesus presented as the second commandment: "You must love your neighbor as yourself" (Matthew 22:39). The Second Vatican Council in Chapter 5 of the Constitution on the Church reiterated the fact that "all the faithful of Christ of whatever rank or status are called to the fullness of the Christian life and to the perfection of charity" (#40).

Further, if marriage is indeed a sacrament, then the married love that a couple have for each other is an effective sign of Christ's love that draws the couple closer to God. Growing intimacy in marriage, rather than "dividing the heart," is meant to bring greater integration of one's life and to deepen one's capacity to love God and others. If this is not true, what does it mean to call marriage a sacrament?

3. While it is agreed that the celibate gives a sign of the kingdom of heaven, all baptized Christians are called to proclaim and further the kingdom of God on this earth and to point to its ultimate fulfillment in the kingdom of heaven. Marriage in its own way gives a sign of the kingdom. The relationship between God and Israel and between Christ and the church are spoken of in the scriptures in terms of a marriage. Our present covenant relationship with God and Christ is brought to fulfillment in heaven. Accordingly, it was fitting that one of the ways in which Jesus spoke of the kingdom of heaven was in terms of a wedding feast (Matthew 22:1-14).

4. Again, no one disagrees with the premise that a priest ought to be available to serve his congregation. However, the assumption that only a celibate can be adequately available is open to challenge on several grounds. First, there are countless married priests of the Eastern rites, Protestant ministers and rabbis who are at least as renowned for their availability and service to their congregations as the average celibate

priest. Second, often in those congregations a married clergyman is perceived as more available for understanding and responding to pastoral problems precisely because he shares an identity with the majority of the congregation who are married. Third, the experience of being married and being a parent, rather than being an obstacle, can be an advantage in running a parish or a diocese. The insight of the author of the first letter to Timothy can still have relevance. Writing about the qualifications of the presiding elder he remarks: "He must be a man who manages his own family well and brings his children up to obey him and be well-behaved; how can any man who does not understand how to manage his own family have responsibility for the church of God?" (1 Timothy 3:4-5).

5. Certainly, dedication as a celibate ought to give an example of Christian chastity. However, the chastity of a married couple and of singles who have either never married or are widowed or divorced is also an inspiration and an example.

Beyond the above objections the following reasons also support a change of law that would allow married persons as well as celibates to be ordained as priests and bishops.

1. For the Christian, celibacy and the sacrament of marriage are charisms, that is, free gifts of the Spirit. Neither charism ought to be a requirement or an obstacle for ordination. Those ought to be ordained who give evidence of an authentic call to priestly ministry, who have a desire to respond to that call, and who possess the qualifications necessary to function effectively as a priest.

Against this it is argued that the church has the right to ordain whomever it wishes. Hence, the call to celibacy can be a prerequisite for recognizing a call to priesthood.

The response to this counterargument is that the Spirit, like the wind, "blows wherever it pleases" (John 3:8). Church authority ought to recognize where there is an authentic call of the Spirit to orders, and not demand as a prerequisite another charism of the Spirit that is not intrinsically linked with priestly ministry. Some would see as applicable to this issue the example of Peter who, despite criticism from some circles, admitted pagans to baptism. "Could anyone refuse the water of baptism to these people, now that they have received the Holy Spirit just as much as we have?" (Acts 10:47). In justifying his conduct later Peter further stated: "I realized then that God was giving them (the pagans) the identical thing he gave to us when we believed in the Lord Jesus Christ; and who was I to stand in God's way?" (Acts 11:17).

2. A sufficient number of priests to serve the Christian community, especially in the celebration of the Eucharist, the sacrament of reconciliation and the anointing of the sick, is more important than an ecclesiastical law. Accordingly, in light of the chronic shortage of priests in many parts of the world, and a growing shortage of priests elsewhere, married persons who experience an authentic call of the Spirit, and who are otherwise qualified for priestly ministry, ought to be ordained. Some would see applicable here the insight enunciated by Jesus: "The sabbath was made for man, not man for the sabbath; so the Son of Man is master even of the sabbath" (Mark 2:27-28).

Those upholding the law of celibacy for priests would counterargue that church law should not be dictated by personnel questions. "Somehow, God will provide," is the hope that is sometimes stated. On the other hand is not such a counter-argument an abdication of human responsibility?

Women Priests?

Two important differences ought to be noted regarding the issue of women priests that distinguish it from the question of married priests. First, the official hierarchy of the Church sees the prohibition of ordaining women priests and bishops as rooted in the will of God, and not merely a matter of human, ecclesiastical legislation. In other words, the official position of the Roman Catholic Church is that while the Pope could, if he wished, change the law of priestly celibacy, he is not free to go contrary to the will of God in the matter of the prohibition of ordaining women. Second, there is a common tradition in the Catholic Church of the East and West regarding the reservation of orders to males.

The following are some of the main arguments proposed for perceiving that it is the divine will that women not be ordained as priests or bishops.

1. Jesus did not admit any women among the Twelve. This is the most often heard argument against women's ordination. It is pointed out that in many ways Jesus broke with the cultural discrimination against women so prevalent in his time. The fact that he did not admit women among the Twelve is a sign, this argument goes, that it was not the will of God to do so. Therefore it would be against the will of Christ to ordain women as priests and bishops today. In light of this argument, opponents to the ordination of women see the ban against women priests to be based on theological reasons and not merely on cultural influences.

2. Jesus did not even make an exception for Mary. Or, as some put it, "Jesus did not even ordain his own mother." This argument takes the first one a step further. For the proponents of this argument, the fact that Jesus declined to admit Mary among the Twelve is a sure sign that no woman can ever be ordained. The assumption here is that if it were theologically possible for women to be ordained, Jesus would have certainly conferred this office on his mother.

3. The fact that for over nineteen and a half centuries neither the church of the East nor the church of the West has ever ordained a woman a priest or a bishop is evidence that the tra-

dition of the church is that such an action would be against the will of God.

4. The priest is a sign of Christ. Since Christ was a male, the priest, in order to be a sign of Christ, must be male. This argument was offered by the Vatican Congregation for the Doctrine of the Faith in section 5 of A Declaration on the Question of the Admission of Women to the Ministerial Priesthood, dated October 15, 1976. The priest is a sign "that must be perceptible and which the faithful must be able to recognize with ease." The document quotes from St. Thomas: "Sacramental signs represent what they signify by natural resemblance." The document then continues: "The same natural resemblance is required for persons as for things: when Christ's role in the Eucharist is to be expressed sacramentally, there would not be this 'natural resemblance' which must exist between Christ and his minister if the role of Christ were not taken by a man: in such a case it would be difficult to see in the minister the image of Christ. For Christ himself was and remains a man."

On the other hand there are a number of major arguments in favor of ordaining women.

1. The mere fact that Jesus did not do something does not necessarily mean it cannot be done. It is true that Jesus chose no women to be among the Twelve. It is also true that he did not choose Romans or Greeks, but only Jews to be among the Twelve. If this argument is carried to its logical conclusion, it would seem that orders would have to be reserved to males of Jewish ethnic background.

Also, there is no indication that there were theological reasons that prevented Jesus from admitting women from the Twelve. It is clear that there were social reasons. The Twelve were called to give witness of their personal experience of Jesus. Women were not considered credible witnesses. One's own mother, it seems, would be considered an even less credible witness.

Finally, as many biblical and theological scholars point out, the offices of priest and bishop as we know them today were a gradual development. While there is a sense in which these offices are a continuation of the mission of the apostles, in another sense the role of the Twelve was unique. Only they were eyewitnesses. In the strict sense it is anachronistic to say that Jesus "ordained" anyone a "priest" or "bishop" in the sense that those terms are known to us today.

2. While it is true that the churches of the East and West have prohibited women from ordination for the entire span of Christian history, the pertinent question is why. Reasons given in ages past were based on the assumption that women were inferior to men. Opponents to women's ordination today reject that assumption but insist that the reasons opposing admission of women to the priesthood are not merely cultural but theological. However, many theologians today do not think that any convincing theological reasons have been offered. Further, in 1976 the Pontifical Biblical Commission in a 12-5 vote stated that scriptural grounds alone are not enough to exclude the possibility of ordaining women.

3. There is agreement about the fact that the priest is a sign of Christ. However, this point must be understood in the context of several other theological insights. First, as already stated a number of times, the entire community of the baptized, women and men, are a priestly people, and hence are called to be a sign of Christ. The uniqueness of the sacramentality of ordained ministry should not obscure the sacramentality of the priesthood of the baptized. The way in which the priest images Christ is related to the way in which all baptized women and men are called to image Christ.

Second, priests and laity in their diverse ways give a sign of Christ by their faith and love and by manifesting the goodness of Christ in their lives and actions. To be a sign of Christ it is not necessary to be similar to Jesus in sex, ethnic background or physical appearance.

4. It is agreed that we cannot speak of an "equal right" to be a priest. The call to priesthood is a gift of the Spirit, and hence a freely given charism. Nevertheless, the refusal to ordain women who sincerely experience the call of the Spirit to priestly ministry raises for many a serious question. What is there about womanhood that automatically disqualifies an otherwise qualified individual from priestly ministry? Until this question is resolved, the credibility of all the other nice things a church says about womanhood is open to challenge.

Summary

In this chapter I have attempted to give a summary of some of the major reasons offered against ordaining married people and women as priests and bishops. I have also stated the reasons why I believe the Church ought to change these prohibitions and admit to orders those persons, married or celibate, women or men, who are qualified and called by the Spirit.

REFLECTION/DISCUSSION QUESTIONS

1. Present your own personal evaluation of each of the arguments and counterarguments offered on each side of the issue of required celibacy for priests.
2. How do you evaluate the different arguments presented on each side of the issue of women's ordination?
3. How would you personally like to see each of these two issues resolved in the future?

Part Seven

CHRISTIAN MARRIAGE

Marriage is a foundational human reality that has its own profound meaning prior to religious considerations. In light of Christian faith, however, marriage takes on the added significance of being a sign of the covenant of love that exists between Christ and his people.

In this section we examine the meaning of the sacramentality of Christian marriage. We will then probe how Christian marriage is related to one's baptismal call. The final chapter discusses the wedding liturgy.

Chapter 29
Sacrament of Christ's Love

From early days Catholics have become familiar with the fact that marriage for Christians is a sacrament. Why this is so and what practical implications the sacramentality of marriage can have for the enrichment of married life are questions that have been less commonly explored.

This chapter examines what is meant by saying that for Christians marriage is a sacrament. It then probes some of the implications that flow from the sacramentality of marriage. The chapter ends with a reflection on several aspects of a sacramental spirituality of married life.

Marriage as Sacrament

The classical New Testament foundation for the Catholic teaching that marriage is a sacrament is Ephesians 5:21-33. In this passage the Pauline author compares the covenantal love relationship between wife and husband with the convenantal love relationship that exists between Christ and the church. In my book, *Marriage: Sacrament of Hope and Challenge,* I have given a rather detailed explanation of this text. It will be sufficient here to point to the main meaning that the text has for

Christian marriage today. In summary it is this: wives and husbands ought to love, regard and treat each other as Christ loves and acts toward us. They ought to respond to each other as the church is called to respond to Christ.

The traditional definition stated that a sacrament is a sign instituted by Christ to give grace. The visible sign in the sacrament of marriage is the living experience of marital love. Marriage, as the Second Vatican Council points out in the Constitution on the Church in the Modern World, is an "intimate partnership of married life and love" (#48). This partnership involves a lifelong commitment on the part of the couple to be for each other and to share themselves with one another in the totality of their lives.

For those with Christian faith Christ brings a new level of meaning to an already rich and significant human experience. Jesus came and gave of himself to humans in an outpouring of friendship and love manifested especially in his teaching and healing ministry, and in his acceptance of death that resulted because of those who rejected him in his ministry. Jesus passed through death into risen life. Now invisible to our mortal eyes, Christ continues to be for us, and to communicate to us his very Spirit. In this way he transforms us, changes our perspective and leads us into new relationship with God.

Because of the reality of Christ, accepted in faith, human marriage for Christians is a sign of Christ's total self-giving. The total commitment in marital love and the transformation we experience in this mutual self-sharing is a sign of Christ's relationship with us and the redemptive transformation he effects in us. Marriage is not just a sign in the sense that it gives witness to the reality of Christ's love. In a very real sense Christ gives of himself to the couple in and through their mutual self-giving. Christ transforms the couple through their own mutual enrichment of each other.

Implications

There are a number of direct consequences that flow from taking seriously the belief that for the Christian marriage is a sacrament, a sign of Christ's love. For our purposes we will cite four of them here.

1. *The quality of the marital relationship is crucial.* Only in a loving relationship can marriage be a living sign of Christ's life-giving, grace-giving love. Hatred and fighting, violent psychological and physical abuse, or mere loveless coexistence under the same roof are countersigns rather than signs of Christ's love. The couple make their lives a sacrament of Christ's covenantal love by daily building the covenant of love that binds them together in growing intimacy and sharing. They grow in this sacramental life to the degree that they allow the quality of Christ's love to inspire and permeate the way they relate to one another. The unique friendship they build in their marriage is a sign of Christ's extraordinary friendship. Through the experience of this friendship, they are drawn by the power of the Spirit into deeper friendship (grace) with God.

2. *The sacramentality of Christian marriage involves faith in Christ.* The human experience of marriage, regardless of how happy and blessed it may be, can only speak to one of Christ if one believes in him. For marriage to be a living sign to the couple of Christ's ongoing life-giving love, the couple must believe in the crucified and risen Christ. The more that Christ means to them in their lives, the more their marital relationship can become for them a concrete embodiment of Christ's love.

3. *The sacrament of marriage is not merely something that happens in the wedding ceremony.* While the wedding ceremony is sacramental, it is only the beginning of a new re-

lationship and a new life together. The entire married life is a
living out of this sacrament. As the marriage grows in the love
of Christ it becomes more sacramental. Or, more accurately,
as the couple grow in Christlike love for each other they grow
as sacraments to each other.

4. *Marriage and the sexual expression of marital love are
intrinsically good and are grace-filled blessings of God.* It
would seem that in light of what has already been said this
truth ought to be obvious. However, people have had trouble
admitting the goodness of marriage, and especially of marital
intercourse. In our American culture sex has often been divorced from love. It has been treated as something "dirty," as
something of which to be ashamed. In the Catholic Church,
for some centuries prior to Vatican II, the bias has been defi-
nitely in favor of celibacy. This has given the impression to
many that married people are considered second class citizens. Since the time of Augustine, marital intercourse was for
the most part justified because of its necessity for bringing
children into the world.

The Second Vatican Council took a far more positive view
of marriage and marital intercourse. Still, one suspects that
some of the negative biases persist. Why, for example, is the
sacrament of marriage seen in the Latin rite as the one insu-
perable barrier to priesthood for an otherwise qualified and
good person? Do we yet tend to justify marital intercourse in
terms of begetting children, and not enough in terms of its own
personally sanctifying and enriching effects?

If we say, as we do, that marriage, as a unique sexual love
relationship, is a grace-giving sign of Christ's love, then marriage must be regarded as having a unique place in the life of
the Church. Married people need to regard and pursue their
marriage as a way to full Christian discipleship. Sexual intercourse in marriage must be perceived as an integral part of the
sacramental sign.

Toward a Spirituality of Married Life

The sacramentality of marriage guides us toward a spirituality of married life. Five aspects of this spirituality can be developed here.

Incarnational

Belief that the word of God became flesh and that Christ is risen from the dead ought to give Christians a new appreciation of the body. To be human is to be embodied spirit, inspirited body. In marriage we accept our body and our sexuality. We express our love, our goodness, our being filled with God's grace in an enfleshed way. Through touch, embrace and the countless physical things we daily do for each other and our children, we express and intensify the spiritual core of our personhood and share in life-giving ways the innermost depths of our being.

Fidelity

In choosing marriage as a way of living out our following of Christ, faithfulness to one another becomes an integral part of the couple's Christian discipleship. This fidelity cannot be seen merely in terms of avoiding adultery. It includes growing in faith and trust in one another. It involves being faithful to the process of becoming increasingly married to each other and of becoming fuller signs of Christ's love. Marital fidelity includes a commitment to grow in all the elements that are important to a happy and enriched married life, such as communication, mutual support, and the effort to keep the romance alive.

Mutual Regard

The oneness in love that exists between a couple implies regarding and loving one's spouse as one does one's own body. This involves respecting one's spouse as an equal person. It also means caring for one's spouse and being sensitive to a spouse's feelings, needs and aspirations.

Generosity and Service

Jesus came and gave of himself in complete love and service. He did not come to be served but to serve. A couple, committed to each other and to the building of their marriage, share the uniqueness of their personal gifts with one another. They are generous in what they give and do for each other. Their service breaks across the boundaries of stereotyped roles that would assign tasks according to gender. In their generosity and service to each other they are freed to reach out beyond the threshold of their home and share their blessings with those less fortunate.

Prayer

Since living the sacrament of marriage involves faith, prayer is essential for building a Christian marriage. Prayer is the human response to God who has already touched us and blessed us. Our prayer in marriage is first of all a prayer of thanksgiving. We are grateful for our lives, our marriage, and one another. We show our gratitude by being open to the continued blessings and graces of God in our married life. Our prayer is also a prayer of trust. We trust that God will continue to be with us and bring to completion the work begun in our marriage. Our prayer is a prayer of continued trust and commitment to one another.

Prayer in marriage takes place on a number of levels. Both persons pray in the depths of their own heart. The couple also deepens the bond with one another by sharing their faith and prayer together. They initiate family prayer which is an important way for the children to "catch" the spirit of their parents' prayer life. The prayerful couple also share their prayer with the wider community. In this way, they enrich the wider worshiping community, and are in turn strengthened by it.

Prayer is not only a response of faith made in time of formal, verbal prayer. Prayer is a lived reality. So in a true sense, the entire married life of the couple, inasmuch as it is lived out as a response in faith, love and trust to Christ and one another, is a prayer.

Summary

Marriage for Christians is a sacrament, that is, a sign of the love that exists between Christ and the church. Living marriage as a sacrament implies some degree of faith in Christ and the effort to build a marriage that reflects mutual love, respect and concern.

DISCUSSION/REFLECTION QUESTIONS

1. What makes a marriage for two Christians a sacrament?
2. In light of your experience describe in some detail a type of marriage that you would consider truly sacramental. Explain why you consider it sacramental.
3. Describe some types of marriages that you would consider countersigns of Christ's life-giving love.
4. Going beyond the author's treatment in this chapter, suggest several other qualities and virtues necessary for living a Christian spirituality of marriage.

Chapter 30
Marriage: Living the Baptismal Call

Frequently during the general intercessions at the Eucharistic liturgy one hears a prayer for an increase of priestly and religious vocations. That, of course, is a valid intercession. However, when was the last time you heard a prayer in church for vocations to Christian marriage? Is the infrequency of such a petition symptomatic of a failure to appreciate marriage as an authentic Christian vocation?

All Christian vocations—priesthood, religious life, single life or marriage—are rooted in the basic vocation received in baptism. In this chapter we consider how marriage for Christians is a call to live out in a unique way the various elements of the baptismal call: to share in the prophetic, priestly and kingly mission of Christ, to be the church of Christ, and to participate in Christ's death and resurrection. What this baptismal call means for all Christians was explored in the section on baptism. Presupposing what was said there, we wish here only to indicate a few ways in which the diverse elements of the baptismal call are lived out in married life.

The Prophetic Dimension

The very fact that marriage is a sacrament, a sign of Christ's love, suggests the prophetic dimension of married life. Through the expression of their marital relationship as a covenant of love, the Christian couple proclaim to one another and to others the meaning of Christ's love. They attest to the central place of Christ in their lives through all of the efforts that they make to live out their Christian discipleship in their marriage. They allow their faith and love of Christ and their acceptance of his value system as reflected in the gospels to inspire and permeate their relationship with one another.

Within this sacramental context of their lives, there are several further specific ways in which the couple participate in the prophetic mission of Christ and the church. First the couple strengthen the faith of each other by sharing together what they truly believe about God, the after-life, the church, their religion. They help one another by sharing and discussing their doubts, confusions, ambivalent feelings and hopes. They confirm each other's struggle to follow Christ by their shared prayer, their example and inspiration, and their belief in one another.

Second, the couple live out the prophetic dimension of their baptism by exercising the primary role in the religious formation of their children. They do this first by creating in the home an atmosphere of faith, trust and love. This atmosphere is built through the regard, concern and belief that the couple manifest toward each other and toward their children. In this way the children come to believe in themselves and in their parents. This important foundation of trusting and loving faith within the home provides the inner security needed to reach out and believe in the God of Jesus Christ, and to build wholesome, faith-filled relationships beyond the threshold of the household. The parents further contribute to the religious formation of their children by sharing with them through word, prayer and example their own faithful following of Christ.

Finally, the couple give witness through their married life to the wider community. Their sharing of faith and the example of their family life, lived out in the spirit of Christian discipleship, provide inspiration, example and hope to the broader circle of friends, neighbors and acquaintances.

The Priestly Dimension

In the section on baptism we referred to what the bishops of Vatican Council II stated about the priesthood of the baptized in #10 of the Constitution on the Church. In describing the ways in which the baptized exercise their priesthood the bishops enumerated the following: participation in the offering of the Eucharist and in the other sacraments, prayer and thanksgiving, the witness of a Christian life, self-sacrifice, and active charity. Following that formula it is clear how marriage provides a unique opportunity for living out the priestly dimension of one's baptismal call. The couple are the ministers of their sacrament of marriage. They lead the family in worship and prayer in the context of the home. Together as a family they become an integral part of the celebration of the Eucharist and other sacraments in the parish community, which itself is made up mostly of families. In unique ways the couple give of themselves to each other in unselfish love. As parents they share the fruit of their love in bringing forth new life, and in the ongoing process of nurturing.

Promoting the Reign of God

To allow God to reign in our lives is to open our minds and hearts to God's inspiration and influence in our decisions and in our relationships. Put more concretely, it means that we allow ourselves to be guided by God's truth, love, peace and justice.

In marriage a couple promote the kingdom (reign) of God by building their marital and parental relationships on honest communication and compassionate love. They work creatively to establish peace and fairness in the home. They respect the equality and rights of each family member as a human person, and seek to provide for the unique needs that each individual has. In this way their manner of dealing with each other is governed not by pettiness, jealousy and self-centeredness, but by the goodness that springs from faith and love of God. Accordingly, the home becomes transformed into a place where God truly dwells. Such a marriage is eschatological, that is, it points to the end time when God's kingdom comes in its fullness.

Domestic Church

In the Constitution on the Church, the Second Vatican Council speaks of the family as the domestic church. There are a number of reasons why this designation is appropriate. First, the family is a unique community bound together by the commitment of marital love on the part of the couple and the blood relationship of the children to their parents and to one another. These bonds are further enhanced in a Christian marriage by the faith and commitment to Christ shared in common by the family members.

Second, the family is a worshiping community. In the home family members share their prayer at meals, at bedtime, and on other occasions. Together they worship in the context of a broader community.

Third, the family is church because it is called to share in the mission of Christ to serve human needs. Family members carry out in a unique way this ministry of service by responding with concern and love to the spiritual, psychological and physical needs of one another. They also share in this mission by opening their own home in hospitality to others, and by reaching out to the needy and poor. They further serve by becoming involved in community efforts to build world peace, and to combat the institutionalized injustices that cause starvation, oppression of the deprived, and the patriarchal discrimination against women.

Participating in Christ's Death and Resurrection

Marriage provides a unique context for sharing in the death and resurrection of Christ. In their marital commitment the wife and husband are called to die to their egocentrism and to be for one another in a new life of covenantal love. Throughout their life they strive in their relationship to die to the bothersome faults and to the dark pockets of jealousy, self-centeredness, intolerance, pettiness and sexism that lurk deeply in the minds and hearts of humans. Through these dyings they achieve new levels of maturity, intimacy and authentic love.

In the rhythm of their relationship the couple also die and rise through many stages of their life together: the early years, the middle years, male and female menopause, and the later stages of their marriage. As parents, the couple must also embrace many experiences of letting go in order to nurture their children toward adulthood. They experience the pain and the joy of ushering their children from babyhood to childhood, and then to the teen years and finally to lives as independent adults.

Even death itself takes on further meaning for the couple. It is not enough to accept the prospect of one's own death; one must also accept all of the dyings that one's death will cause to spouse and children. One must also embrace the prospect of the death of a spouse and the dyings that will bring. But the baptized Christian does so, believing with Psalm 89 that "love is built to last forever," and believing that from all the dyings new life emerges both for those left behind on earth, as well as for the one who goes on to the life we call heaven.

Summary

For the Christian, marriage is a specific way of life in which one is called to live out the baptismal vocation. In the context of married life and of parenthood, the couple share in the prophetic, priestly, and kingly mission of Christ. They also form Christian community in the home and participate in the death and resurrection of Christ.

Discussion/Reflection Questions

1. In your opinion, what percentage of Christian couples approach their marriage as a divine vocation rooted in their baptismal call? Please explain your answer. If your answer is on the negative side, what can be done in religious education and formation programs and in the life of the church to sensitize people to the vocational dimension of marriage?
2. How can a couple, in their preparation for marriage, help one another choose this sacrament as a way in which they can together live out their baptismal commitment?
3. Suggest several concrete ways in which the family as domestic church and the wider parish community can enrich one another.

Chapter 31
The Wedding Liturgy

While the sacrament of marriage is far more than merely the nuptial ceremony, the wedding liturgy is a sacrament and marks the couple's initiation into this sacramental way of married life. In this chapter we will reflect on the present wedding liturgy. We will then offer suggestions on how a couple can prepare their own marriage ceremony. Finally we will reflect on possible future liturgical developments.

The Wedding Liturgy

The rite of marriage may take place either during the celebration of the Eucharist or outside of it. When the Eucharist is celebrated, the rite of marriage is conducted after the liturgy of the word, and the nuptial blessing is given after the Lord's Prayer. When the rite of marriage is celebrated outside of the Eucharist, it includes a liturgy of the word.

In the actual rite of marriage, after the priest makes some introductory remarks, he questions the couple regarding their freedom and their intent to get married. Then the couple declare their consent to marry each other. After the rings are blessed, the couple present them to one another.

In expressing their consent the wife and husband each state: "I, N., take you, N., to be my wife (husband). I promise to be true to you in good times and in bad, in sickness and in health. I will love you and honor you all the days of my life" (Rite of Marriage, #45). This consent can also be given by having the priest put it in question form and having the spouses answer "I do." It seems, however, more symbolic for the spouses to declare their consent rather than to give short answers to someone else's questions.

In the United States the familiar form from a past era may still be used: "I, N., take you, N., for my lawful wife (husband), to have and to hold, from this day forward, for better, for worse, for richer, for poorer, in sickness and in health, until death do us part" (#45). While both formulas of consent leave a lot to be desired, the first one seems more positive and hence preferable to the second.

In the ring ceremony the priest first blesses the rings with these words: "May the Lord bless these rings which you give to each other as the sign of your love and fidelity" (#47). Two variations of this blessing are provided.

> Lord, bless these rings which we bless in your name.
> Grant that those who wear them
> may always have a deep faith in each other.
> May they do your will
> and always live together
> in peace, good will, and love.
>
> We ask this through Christ our Lord (#110).

> Lord,
> bless and consecrate N. and N.
> in their love for each other.
> May these rings be a symbol
> of true faith in each other,
> and always remind them of their love.
>
> We ask this through Christ our Lord (#111).

In wedding liturgies that take place outside of the Eucharist, the blessing of the rings is followed by general intercessions, the nuptial blessing, and a concluding prayer and blessing. When the rite of marriage is celebrated during Mass, the priest proceeds with the Eucharist immediately after the rings are blessed and exchanged.

Planning the Wedding Liturgy

As ministers of the sacrament of marriage the couple ought to participate as fully as possible in the preparation and design of the wedding liturgy, based on the options provided by the new rite. There are several good books geared at aiding the couple in this endeavor. Only some basic guidelines and suggestions are highlighted here.

1. *The couple must keep in mind that the wedding rite is not performed by the priest.* It is not something that is happening to them. The bride and groom themselves are the ministers of this sacrament. As far as possible, within the limits of what is allowed in the present rite, the couple ought to appear clearly as the ministers of this sacrament, with the priest as a witness to the central action that they are performing.

In a church wedding this means that the couple ought to have the central position in the sanctuary during the actual rite of marriage. The witness should be off to the side witnessing, not presiding. The faces of the couple ought to be visible to the entire congregation. The words they say in the consent and the exchange of rings need to be proclaimed in a way that is easily audible to the entire congregation. If necessary, the loudspeaker system should be used. When the marriage rite is performed within Mass, it is suggested that during the Eucharist, the couple's kneelers be positioned in a way in which more than their backs are observable to the congregation.

2. *Any semblance of male dominance and patriarchalism is best avoided.* It is only in recent decades in America that our consciousness has been raised to how wrong it is that our notion of marriage be influenced by prejudices of male supremacy and male dominance. While in America we no longer believe, as earlier centuries did, that the husband owns his wife, we did buy into the culture-bound male bias that the husband was "head of his wife." In our efforts to move away from that prejudice, the wedding ceremony ought to reflect the true equality that the wife and husband enjoy as human beings and as co-partners who together will create a new home, a new family.

The first place where this equality can be reflected is in the wedding procession. The practice of the father (or some other man, in place of the father) walking the bride down the aisle and then handing her over to the husband appeals to many for sentimental reasons. However, the practice harkens back to a partriarchal age when the father transferred ownership of his daughter to her new owner, her husband.

Because of this, feminist sensitivities call for alternative models of procession. Four possible models can be mentioned here. (a) Both the bride's family and the groom's family process down the aisle together, followed by the bridal party and the bride and groom. (b) If the wedding is small (for example, thirty or forty people) all gather at the doors of the church and process in together: guests, immediate families, bride and groom, in that order. Perhaps they could even sing an appropriate hymn while processing. (c) The members of the bridal party, followed by the bride alone, process down the middle aisle. The groom could process from the side, along the front of the church. The bride and groom would then meet in front of the altar. (d) The family of the bride, the bridal party, and the bride process down the middle aisle. The family of the groom, the best man, and the groom process from the side, along the front of the church. When the processions meet in the front of the church, the bride kisses her parents, the groom kisses his parents, and they walk away from their families and meet each other by the altar. What these and similar models have in common is that they avoid any appearance of male-dominated sexism.

The second place where sexism ought to be avoided is in the scripture readings. The texts that reflect a male-dominated culture of the past are best left unread at a wedding. Unless such texts can be given lengthy explanations, the only thing most people will hear will be the sexist overtones.

Finally, in selecting from the options provided, one can avoid the prayer and blessing that assign the "care of the home" to the wife. Hopefully, wife and husband will embrace together their mutual responsibility in this regard. Let's pray that they *both* do.

3. *The wedding ceremony can be kept simple so as to bring out its sacramental dimensions.* An extravagant spectacular might cater to social status, but clouds the meaning of the event. A simplicity in the wedding ceremony that is compatible with aesthetic taste gives a sign that the couple do not place a priority on materialism and consumerism but are more concerned about the spiritual and personal dimensions of their relationship. A simple ceremony, unencumbered by distracting extravagance, allows the religious meaning of the service to be clearly manifest. It also makes it possible for the wedding to be a ceremony in which all can participate rather than a spectacular to be observed.

4. *The couple ought to familiarize themselves with the optional readings, prayers and blessings that are available for their wedding.* This will enable the couple to design a ceremony appropriate for them. A good marriage preparation program ought to help the couple in this endeavor.

5. *It is very helpful if the couple put together a printed or mimeographed program containing the parts of the ceremony in which the congregation can participate.* This includes the order of the ceremony, the hymns and the responses.

6. *The bride and the groom ought to have an active role in as much of the wedding ceremony as possible.* They could say a few words of welcome at the beginning of the ceremony and/or some words of thanks at the end. They could do some of the readings and the intercessions. If the wedding ceremony takes place within the Eucharist, the couple could minister the Eucharistic bread and wine to each other and aid in the distribution of Communion to the congregation. An active role helps accentuate the fact that the couple are the ministers of the sacrament of marriage and the hostess and host of the wedding celebration.

7. *Some creative personal touches can be incorporated into the liturgy of marriage.* Even when the marriage rite takes place outside of Mass the greeting of peace could be included. A renewal of baptismal commitment would be appropriate prior to declaring the marriage consent. This could help show the connection between the two sacraments.

A candle ceremony at the end of the marriage rite can be very symbolic. The lit paschal candle, symbolizing the risen Christ, could be in a prominent place near the altar from the beginning of the ceremony. After the exchange of rings the bride and groom light a special marriage candle from the paschal candle. (Or, as a variation of this, the parents of the bride light their candle from the paschal candle. The parents of the groom do likewise. The bride and groom light their marriage candle from the two candles of their parents.) The bride and groom then distribute candles, lit from their marriage candle, to each of the guests. These candles could be simply engraved, and kept as a remembrance of the occasion. An appropriate song could accompany this ceremony. A suitable prayer could introduce or conclude it.

The symbolism of such a ceremony is quite evident. The light of Christ's love comes to us first through our parents' love. The fire of our own love is meant to bring greater love into the lives of others.

8. *Parents and other family members can be invited to participate in the readings and intercessions.* If required, they could also be appointed to distribute Communion.

9. *There ought to be some continuity of simplicity and aesthetic taste between the ceremony and the reception.* Senseless or distasteful gestures such as throwing rice, scribbling suggestive vulgarities on the car, and tossing out the garter seem inappropriate and out of line with a sacramental celebration.

Possible Future Developments

In the Constitution on the Sacred Liturgy the bishops of Vatican Council II stated: "The marriage rite now found in the Roman Ritual is to be revised and enriched in a way which more clearly expresses the grace of the sacrament and the duties of the spouses" (#77). Certainly the new revised rite of marriage represents a definite step toward achieving this goal. While the perfect wedding liturgy will never be achieved, the church must continue to revise and enrich the marriage rite so that it even more clearly reflects the theological meaning of Christian marriage. Here our intent is merely to provide a few reflections on two areas in which the present rite could be improved in order to achieve more fully the goal set down by Vatican II.

First, the rite needs to be further revised in a way that

will bring out more clearly the role of the bride and groom as ministers of this sacrament. While on a theoretical level many Catholics know that the priest is only the witness and the couple the ministers, the public perception is quite different. "Father So-and-So married us" is what one ordinarily hears. Many wedding announcements in the Sunday paper speak of the priest or clergyman as "performing the wedding ceremony."

Indeed the present ceremony reinforces this false notion. Except for the declaration of consent and the exchange of rings, which too often cannot be heard beyond the sanctuary, all of the other details of the ceremony point to the priest as presider and performer, rather than as witness. He stands at the central position before the altar facing the congregation. He introduces and concludes the rite, says almost all the prayers, and imparts the blessings. He even overshadows the consent and exchange of rings by his dominant presence, his words, and more often than not his "stage directions." When one recalls that prior to the Middle Ages the presence of the priest as a witness was not even required, it is clear what a development of the clerical role has taken place at weddings.

It would be soundly theological for the church to provide a wedding rite that would be performed solely by the couple in the presence of a priest as witness. This means that the welcome, the explanation of the significance of the ceremony, the prayers and blessings would be conducted by the couple. The readings and some of the intercessions would be done by family members. What the priest would do would be to witness. If one feels that "the rings must be blessed by the priest," this could be done privately before the ceremony.

It may be argued that at present many, if not most, couples would be uncomfortable, and perhaps incapable of presiding at their own wedding. Because this might be true, at least at first, my proposal is that this revised rite be offered as an option. As more people experience this kind of a wedding ceremony, the problem would be alleviated. The difficulty will be further minimized as more lay people get used to performing other public liturgical functions such as lector and Eucharistic minister. Training for conducting the wedding ceremony could also become an integral part of marriage preparation programs. Such training could prove to be an excellent vehicle for explaining the theological significance of the sacrament of Christian marriage.

The second area in which the marriage rite needs further revision is in the formula of consent and the prayers and blessings. The new formula of consent in the revised rite is an improvement over the old formula. It speaks of promise, love and honor. However, it leaves out much of the rich meaning of marriage, and entirely neglects the Christian dimension. While it speaks of "taking" the other as one's spouse, it says nothing of giving oneself to the other in marital commitment and love. It omits all reference to Christ, to the sacramentality of marriage, and to the community and ministerial dimensions of Christian marriage. To put it another way, an atheist could recite this formula without any difficulty.

Obviously, no one formula can contain all of the significance of Christian marriage. However, the rite of consent would be greatly improved if there were provided a number of options from which to choose. The optional forms of consent could, in varying degrees, highlight the specifically Christian dimensions of marriage for a baptized couple who take seriously their Christian commitment.

A greater variety of options for the prayers and nuptial blessings would also enrich the rite of marriage. These ought to be formulated in such a way as to underscore further the Christian and personalist aspects of marriage.

Summary

Following the directive of the Second Vatican Council, the church has provided a revised rite of marriage which certainly marks an improvement over the recent past. Within the present rite there are many ways in which a couple can make this a very meaningful liturgy. It is hoped, nevertheless, that the church will continue to revise and enrich the wedding liturgy in ways that will more richly reflect the biblical and theological meaning of marriage, and that will inspire a dedication to married life as an authentic Christian vocation.

REFLECTION/DISCUSSION QUESTIONS

1. Explain your personal evaluation of each of the suggestions made in the second section of this chapter, "Planning the Wedding Liturgy." What further suggestions would you have?
2. Suggest specific ways in which a couple might renew their marriage commitment on each anniversary, in the context of a home prayer service and celebration.
3. Regarding possible future developments in the wedding liturgy, what further ways do you think the role of bride and groom as ministers of the sacrament could be more clearly manifested in the rite of marriage?
4. Write a formula of declaration of marital consent that you think would reflect the meaning of Christian marriage better than does the present rite.

Conclusion

This book has addressed itself to the deep kind of questioning so often raised by the young—and the not so young. "Why do I need to go to the sacraments?" "If I lead a good life, why is liturgical worship necessary?" "What relevance do sacraments have for everyday living?"

The key to understanding the sacraments is to begin not with "the seven sacraments" but with the basic sacramental realities of life and friendship. To experience love is already to be encountered by God. If we do not find God in the daily living of friendships, how do we find God in sacraments? If, as Christians, we do not discover Christ in a compassionate community of fellow believers and disciples, how do we discover him in baptism, or reconciliation, or the Eucharist?

The sacraments flow from the rich experience of Christ in our lives and in our Christ-filled communities. In turn, our encounters with Christ in the sacraments inspire and grace us to drink and share more deeply of the blessings of God incarnated in the daily experiences of our earthly lives. Such drinking and sharing not only transform us now, but also bring us closer to the end fulfillment when there will be "a new heaven and a new earth" where God will dwell among us in the fullest possible way (Revelation 21:1-3).

Further Readings

There is no attempt here to provide a bibliography that could only prove overwhelming to the average reader. We merely list several books that will be useful for those who wish to pursue their study of the sacraments.

Bausch, William J. *A New Look at the Sacraments.* Mystic, CT: Twenty-Third Publications, 1983.

Cooke, Bernard. *Sacraments and Sacramentality.* Mystic, CT: Twenty-Third Publications, 1983.

Guzie, Tad. *The Book of Sacramental Basics.* Ramsey, N.J.: Paulist Press, 1981.

Hellwig, Monika K. (editor). *Message of The Sacraments,* Vols. 1–7. Wilmington: Michael Glazier, Inc., 1983.

McBrien, Richard P. *Catholicism,* Chapters XXI and XXII. Minneapolis: Winston Press, 1980.

Roberts, William P. *Marriage: Sacrament of Hope and Challenge.* Cincinnati: Saint Anthony Messenger Press, 1983.

Schillebeeckx, Edward. *Christ the Sacrament of the Encounter with God.* New York: Sheed and Ward, 1963.

Taylor, Michael J. (editor). *The Sacraments: Readings in Contemporary Sacramental Theology.* New York: Alba House, 1981.